From the Shankill to the Shenandoah

1603 JAMES IV (" I) SUCCEEDED ELIZ.

Arthur Woods was born in Birmingham in 1920, and served as a soldier in World War II from 1939 to 1946.

As an international salesman in heavy industry, he worked in Western Europe, behind the Iron Curtain in Eastern Europe, in the Middle East and in the USA. He has written a memoir, with a rich mixture of travel, history, politics and work, entitled *A Huckster - 50 Years on the Roads of East and West Europe and Elsewhere*.

He has also written an investigation into the life of St. Paul and his posthumous effect on the Christian faith - *Paul of Tarsus: An enigma Enshrouded in a Mystery*.

699   1663 STAPLE ACT
WOOLENS ACT
1703   TEST ACT   (Queen Anne)

596 HENRY OF NAVARRE
PARIS IS WORTH A MASS .

1703 (TEST ACT)

572

Part of the Province of Ulster

From the Shankill

to the

Shenandoah:

A personal view of the Scotch Irish in America

Arthur Woods

The Grimsay Press

The Grimsay Press
an imprint of
Zeticula
57 St Vincent Crescent
Glasgow
G3 8NQ
Scotland.

http://www.thegrimsaypress.co.uk
admin@thegrimsaypress.co.uk

First published 2007

Every effort has been made to trace possible copyright holders and to obtain their permission for the use of any copyright material. The publishers will gladly receive information enabling them to rectify any error or omission for subsequent editions.

ISBN-10   1 84530 031 9 Paperback
ISBN-13   978 184530 031 9 Paperback

Acknowledgements

My thanks go to

Nick Woods, who gave me the idea for this book, and for part of the title.

Marian Tokarski, who transferred my childish script onto the word processor, quickly, accurately and patiently.

The many authors, now too numerous to mention individually, who have informed my thinking, and consequently left in my head ideas and information which now come together in this volume. Without their unknowing help, this book would not have happened. Any errors, of course, are mine alone.

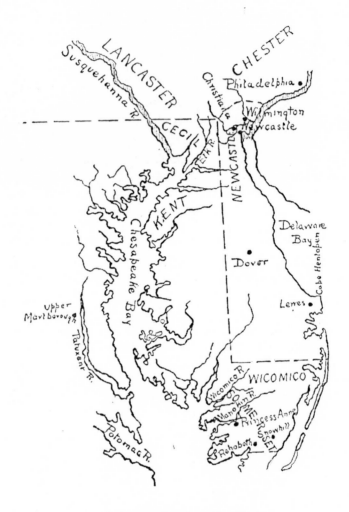

Delaware Bay Landing Ports

Contents

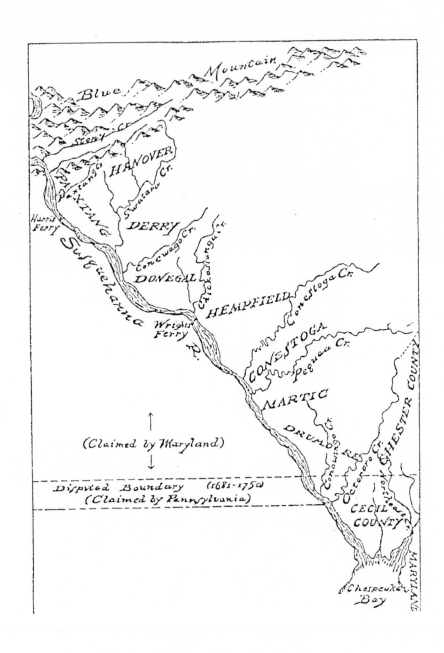

Original Townships along the Susquehanna River,
Lancaster County, 1739

Maps

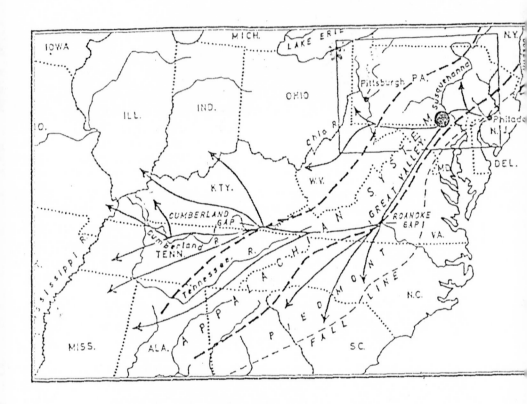

The Cumberland Cradle, the seed-bed of Scots-Irish migration to the Cumberland Valley

Author's Preface

To understand the Shankill, a potted history of Belfast helps. After the Ulster Plantation which started in 1610, Belfast changed from a small fishing and rural community into a small centre of industry, starting with the industrialization of the linen industry, as it moved away from the domestic and cottage Production of that wonderful cloth, and continued into the manufacture of equipment to service the linen Producers. By 1700 the town had a population of about 8000. By 1806 it had grown to 22,000 and to 350,000 in 1900, despite the famine of 1846-50 and emigration, which cost the present Six Counties of Ulster about 170,000 people. The population increase by 1900 was to some extent due to Catholics coming up from the South and West to replace those who had left for America or died in the potato famine. Before the famine and emigration, Belfast had few Catholics; after, the balance changed, and the troubles began.

Ship building began in 1850 and Belfast developed into the largest shipyard in the world; the *Titanic* was built there. Because of industry and the jobs it creates, the Catholic population between 1926 and 1961 increased by 18% while in the Irish Republic it fell by 3%. Hence the gap between the two sects of the Christian Religion narrowed further though the Protestants still had a comfortable majority. The increase was mostly among the working classes; most of the skilled jobs went to the Protestants, while the unskilled and generally low paid work was done by the Catholics.

There have been ten serious riots in Belfast in which many people were killed: 1813, 1825, 1857, 1864, 1872, 1886, 1898, 1920-2, 1935 and 1968-9. The foundations of what was to happen from 1969 for the next 30 years were well laid and rock hard. The area of working class Catholics in the Falls Road is virtually surrounded by working class Protestants of a pronounced sectarian nature. The battleground was determined by this.

The Catholic position was weak when, in 1969, they started *again* to demonstrate for better housing, more jobs without discrimination, and an end to political jerrymandering. The Protestants, whose iron hand was never in a velvet glove, were determined to maintain possession and authority in all those fields, and protested vigorously and, when necessary, physically. The Irish Republican Army, the

IRA, which began to be a force to be reckoned with in 1919, first against the British soldiery then in the Civil War of 1922, when Partition began, had become moribund. In 1969 when the serious fighting began, the young men of the IRA broke away to form splinter groups, like the Provisionals, the Provos, and their aim was to make what they termed "war" against the British to make them leave Ulster, so that it could be united with the rest of Ireland. It had only ever been one nation before and *that* was under the British.

The British Army, which had not been in Ulster since World War II, started to return, as the Catholics asked for protection against the Protestants, and their quasi military force, the 'B' Specials. As the Army did not attack the Protestants, the Catholics turned hostile and rioting became worse. The Army was forced to increase to 22,000 by 1976. To put that in perspective, the British never had more than 30,000 soldiers in India to govern five hundred million until World War II.

Attitudes changed. It was no longer "good old Tommy, come here to wallop the Protestants" but insults, spitting and jeering at the troops. A favourite apocryphal story says that when the Army made a routine car search in Belfast in a middle class suburb they would say to the driver "Excuse, me, Sir, would you mind if I looked in the boot of your car?" but in the Catholic Falls Road it changed to "Open your fucking boot, you bastard, and quick!" I hope this story, though amusing, is untrue. But it might have depended on whether or not a soldier had been killed the previous night. Between 1969 and 1998, 3,637 people were killed in Ulster, of which 465 were soldiers and 272 policemen. There were 45,000 wounded and 36,000 shootings. Over the 30 years of the Troubles, 300,000 British soldiers served in Ulster. 70% of the butchers' bill is owed by the IRA, the rest to the Protestant Loyalists. The cost to Britain is about £100 million, or 180 billion dollars. By far the greatest number of deaths, by street shootings, and bombs, usually in cars parked in busy thoroughfares to kill the greatest number, took place in Belfast.

When Rudyard Kipling wrote in one of his poems, "East is East and West is West, and never the twain shall meet," he was writing about India, but he could have had Belfast in mind. The Protestants in the Shankill are to the East of the Catholics on the

Falls Road, with a hatred between them no less than that between a Scotch Irish frontiersman and an Indian in Pennsylvania in the 1760's. Moreover in an attempt to keep the two tribes apart, an iron wall was built of corrugated iron embedded in concrete; like a mini Berlin Wall but much more dangerous. There was civil war in Ulster working class areas fed by sectarian and religious hatred, and fear on the part of the Protestants that Britain will betray them, and encourage Ulster to rejoin Ireland, the Irish Republic. But the Protestants will never accept the suzerainty of the Dublin Government nor the Pope of Rome.

From a primitive start, the IRA became highly sophisticated in weaponry secret organisation over the years, obtaining financial aid from Arab and Communist countries, and millions of dollars from Catholic Irish Americans. By comparison, the Protestants were paupers. The violence of the IRA was countered by savage brutality on the part of the Protestants, particularly against Catholic civilians believed to be giving shelter and assistance to the IRA. Thus was born the legend of the Shankill, and the 'Shankill Butchers'.

The 'Shankill Butchers' may well be the direct descendants of those immigrants that came over from Scotland in 1610 up to the 1770's to form the Ulster Plantation, where they suffered greatly in every way that comes to mind. Hated by the native Irish they frequently had to kill in self-defence, to hold their land and protect their families. Nurture perhaps more than nature made them hard and ruthless, as they discovered, when they found themselves on the Pennsylvanian Frontier, fighting and defending family and his land.

Arthur Woods,
April, 2007

King William of Orange, victor at the Battle of the Boyne in 1690, went into a pub a few days later for a pint. Sitting with his feet up and happy, he saw an old bloke in a corner with his head in his hands. A kindly man, he thought he would cheer the old feller up, so he went over, and saw it was King James.

"Hello, father-in-law. How's it goin'?"

James looked up dolefully. "What do you think, after the walloping you gave me at the Boyne? I feel like topping myself."

William shook his head. "Come on now, father-in-law. This is Ireland. Everyone will have forgotten the Boyne in a couple of weeks."

A popular joke in the Orange Lodges of Ireland in 1998

The English never remember.
The Irish never forget.

Prologue: Dalriada

Malruabh "The bold red-headed one," they say landed on the Island of Skye in the Hebrides from Ulster and preached in the 6th century AD. The Skye people are regarded as quintessentially Scottish, and many of the older people speak the Gaelic today, and are famous for their Presbyterian piety. But Scotland belonged to the future, and in Malruabh's time the North was held by the Celts, that is, the Picti. The Irish tribe known as the Scoti was beginning to fashion the Lordship of DALRIADA in what is now Argyllshire, and from which Scotland emerged. There is a hill fort called Dunadd on Skye, believed to have been the Capital of DALRIADA, a place of coronations and festivals.

The first written inscriptions around here show that the Scoti were linguistically and culturally part of Ireland; and a 7th or 8th century cross about 1 mile from Dunadd reads "XRT REITON" or, "In the name of Christ, Reiton. A stone inscribed at Poltulloch reads "Cronan", a common Irish name from the 9th century, and is written in ogham script, an early Irish system of writing.

The Scoti absorbed the Picti in the 840's under Kenneth MacAlpin, the better to resist the marauding Vikings.

The cult of Malruabh went on to survive the influence of the Norsemen, and the English from the South. It survived the religious cataclysm of the Reformation when the Lowlands were preached at by the firebrand John Knox, and the Gaelic language of the Irish remained predominant. So when the Scoti slipped to and fro across the narrow sea to Ulster for nearly 1000 years up to the Plantation, they spoke only Gaelic.

"The Ulster Plantation was a movement in a single cultural continuum, bringing the descendants of the original Irish tribes originally settled in Dalriada back to the land of their ancestors." Thus wrote Padraig D. Snodaigh in his "Hidden Ulster".

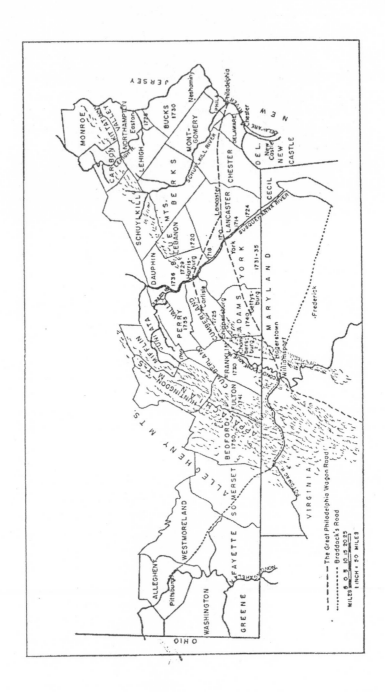

Pennsylvania: The Great Valley

1. The Beginning

It is less than 10,000 years since the English Channel (or *La Manche* as the French more humbly call it) was formed and the section of Europe now called the United Kingdom was separated forever from the European Peninsula. By 3200 BC the Peninsula was inhabited by hunter/gatherers who later became urbanised in a primitive fashion, living by agriculture. This became normal as far North as Latitude 62°N, which lies 100 miles or so north of the northern-most tip of Scotland.

About the same time as the English Channel was formed, the narrow causeway that joined the north-eastern point of Ulster to Scotland was submerged, leaving a channel no more than 12 miles wide separating Ireland from Scotland, creating an island of political turbulence riven by tribal fighting, then fierce and cruel wars, from earliest records to the present day.

There is plenty of evidence of peoples striving towards civilisation in this pre-historic Europe, but none more dramatic than Stonehenge in Southern England, where the skills of the engineers of Stonehenge contributed to transport the eighty bluestones – each of 50 tons or more –150 miles from the distant mountains of Prescelly in South Wales and to erect them with such precision that awestruck observers have imagined them to be the working parts of a sun computer. Moreover, carvings of axes and daggers found there resembling objects taken from the graves of Mycenae in ancient Greece gave rise to speculation of a Mediterranean connection.

Stonehenge is carbon dated at about 1850 BC plus or minus 200 years. In a village called Slane in County Meath in Ireland is a burial mound in which there are passages leading to graves. The main chamber is lined with cut stone. At the mound entrance in the top of it, there is what is known as a roof box. The mound faces the south east; if the sky is clear on the Winter Solstice of 22nd December, the rising sun shines through the box to light up the shallow pits of stone in which had been laid the part cremated bones of the dead. Elsewhere similar burial mounds with their passages to graves have been found; 40 or more have been found in this area of Slane called New Grange. New Grange architectural workings date from at least 3000 BC, a thousand years earlier than Stonehenge.

The creators of these monumental constructs were no ordinary people. You needed some knowledge of mathematics, astronomy, architecture and organised labour to show such respect for your dead. This was the time when the ancient Egyptians, along with a written language, were building magnificent tombs and pyramids. No evidence of language has yet been discovered belonging to this clearly articulate people.

It has been confidently asserted that the first inhabitants of what George Bernard Shaw, the great Irish playwright, called "John Bull's Other Island" (1904) arrived at least 3000 years before the birth of Christ. But where from? The great migrations into Europe always came from the East and South East; and then onwards Westwards until the seas were reached. That was the route of the Celts who stopped off and remained in such places as Portugal, Galicia in north-west Spain, Brittany in France, Wales and Scotland. The Celts were in fact the first great tribe or people in Europe; but they did not reach Ireland, in the west, until 700 BC, where they found a people at least as cultured as themselves, who had been resident for 2000 years or more. They were a robust lot; in their early days more inclined towards destruction than construction., they probably destroyed much before settling down to become a civilised and creative nation.

Before reaching the Western seas and settling in various places in Europe they were a running sore to the Roman legions. Fighting to the Celt seemed nothing more than a bloody pursuit, concerned neither with principle nor gain. They were dangerous thugs with a disposition to what is called today asymmetric warfare: shoot and scoot. Making up the rules as you go, always outnumber the enemy at the point of battle, never giving him a chance to assemble a superior force. However permanent they settled down, it was always dangerous to antagonise them; the love of dispute and the fight was never far below the surface. Their descendants in the English-speaking countries are clearly of the same blood and bone in their love of rough, intimidatory sports such as boxing, rugby and football.

The earliest possessors of Ireland, this much troubled isle, for 2000 years or more before the Celts arrived were either destroyed by them or assimilated during many centuries, leaving virtually no trace of their origins save the stone burial mounds in County Meath. It could never be said that they were colonialists; they were the only occupiers of Ireland against whom that jibe could not be hurled. The Celts were the first and by no means the last, and they settled down as agriculturalists, workers in metals, wood and other media, including gold and silver. This must have been a golden age in which physical prowess, love of art and learning were all part of an articulate society, and which led, no doubt, to Ireland earning the soubriquet of "Land of Saints and Scholars".

From sagas passed on by succeessive generations, they would have learned of their turbulent history, wandering over thousands of miles from the East before reaching the security of Ireland. Protected from enemies by the violent, dangerous seas, they might even have thought that Paradise on Earth had been reached. The seas certainly kept out the Romans, never great sailors. After the first taste of Britain by Julius Caesar in 55 BC, to test the temperature of the water, it was nearly a further 100 years, in 43 AD before the Emperor Claudius bloodily conquered most of the land south of the Celtic Scots.

Had the Romans got over their fear of salt water and risked the passage to the Eastern shores of Ireland, landing perhaps in the area of what is now Dublin, or perhaps a little more south west, around Cork, the history of the Emerald Isle would have been quite different. With little knowledge of latitude and none of longitude, of course, they could easily have missed Ireland completely, and ended up somewhere between Rhode Island and South Carolina. Then where would we have all been during the next 2000 years? This is not as fanciful as it sounds. One thousand years before the birth of Christ, the Phoenicians, courageous and skilful mariners, sailed from the Lebanon in the Eastern Mediterranean 3,000 miles to Cornwall in Britain to buy tin.

The Gaelic Irish: Land of Saints and Scholars

Few known societies have been given the opportunity to evolve with such minor interference and for so long as that of Gaelic Ireland. Only its predecessors – whom it destroyed – had been a major exception. Tradition and legend with no external clash or stimulation consolidated its long, lonely but animated history. It was a geophysical and cultural time capsule. Fragmentation was one of its weaknesses, with no central government, as it adhered to the tribal structures of its forebears. There was a common language, common customs and culture, but tribal self-interest was paramount.

When invaders came – the Danes, the Normans, the English, their first view may have been "Do we eject them, or hire them to help overcome our tribal enemies?" The confusion of the invader can be understood. There was chaos, but controlled chaos. Despite the continual tribal fighting, the Celts were in many ways ahead of their time.

Each tribe had its own body of customary law, passed on orally from one generation of learned lawyer to the next. Land was collectively owned, and not even the King had the right to dispose of any. Pastoral and agricultural, it was the source of all collective wealth.

There was no hereditary leader; the King was elected from the tribal aristocracy. Not that the choice was not bloodily disputed sometimes. A professional middle class of Druids (priests), judges, historians, poets, bards and physicians had respect and authority; similar to that of modern Civil Servants. The proletariat was divided into free people and slaves captured in battle, augmented by slaves taken in amphibious raids on the main lands of Wales and England. The fighting, except when the monarchy was in dispute, tended to be over cattle raiding and the search for slaves. But formal battle tended to be asymmetric incursions in the manner of the Condottieri of Renaissance Italy. Such forays were commemorated by the bards and poets to sustain tribal morale. Skilled in the creative use of gold, silver and other metals to make beautiful artefacts, their poets, storytellers and artists were greatly honoured.

Their spirituality, though pagan, showed a belief in something more enduring than material matters and ruthless acquisition. This provided a sound foundation in the acceptance of the Christian faith, when it came in the early 5th century AD. Ireland was full of English innovators, and the most famous was St Patrick. Captured as a boy in England, he was seven years a slave in Antrim. He escaped back to England, ordained a priest and returned to Ulster to proselytise Christianity. There was success – in time, but there were other missionary collaborators at work. Pope Celestine was so impressed with the Faith's strong foothold in Ireland, he sent Palladius as the first Irish bishop in 431AD. St Patrick spent many years in Ireland, among other places.

Christianity, along with the Latin tongue, brought Ireland into the community of European Catholic countries. it was considered to be a rich source of devout priests and monks who spread the faith from Scotland to the Alps, even to the Court of Charlemagne. No wonder it was spoken of affectionately as: the Land of Saints and Scholars.

16

2. Religion in Scotland

Christianity is generally accepted as arriving in Scotland in the sixth century, by way of the Irish monk Saint Columba (521-597) on the Western Island of Iona, which became the seat of his mission work among the Picts and the Scots. There is evidence that Celts reached the island of Skye at least a century earlier to preach Christianity.

Scotland is as far north as St Petersburg and Moscow. This put it very much on the extreme edge of Christendom and was thus untouched by the maelstrom, the chaos, that tore the early Church apart, after the death of Paul, during the first to the eighth centuries AD. No schismatics such as the Docetes, the Gnostics, the Donatists, the Monophysites, to name just a few, arrived to dispute the nature of Jesus. Was he man or divine? Was the Son and God made of the same substance? Was God in three parts, God the Father, God the Son and God the Holy Ghost? Such heresies tore the Roman world into tatters, causing wars and heavy casualties. Paul would have been horrified at the aftermath of his teachings. Later, John Knox had no such doubts. Scotland was fortunate perhaps in having few intellectuals. Few of the gentry could read either.

Religion languished for several centuries. Wars devastated the Scottish Lowlands; raids by the Vikings, Angles, Normans and, later, the English, did not encourage a poorly educated priesthood and an indifferent Catholic hierarchy to attend to the spiritual needs of the peasantry up until the early twelfth century. King David I gave some structure to the Catholic religion; he set out to establish discipline and stability, with several bishoprics; he gave them a lot of land, and encouraged church building and fine houses. A system was thus created; all those within it owed their authority to him. The Bishops and the other church functionaries would then command the common people by a mixture of piety, charity and severity. He brought in many learned English monks and encouraged the building of monasteries and convents. He tried to suppress the pious Culdees, an Irish/Scottish religious order which maintained Celtic speech and customs, from the 7th until the 13th century, following the teachings of Iona rather than Rome. David's Anglicanisation of Scotland, or at least his attempt to do so, antagonised the people.

The Church as a monopoly religion behaved as monopolies always do: it became corrupt, arrogant and discouraged disagreement. Its powers, its wealth through gifts, wills and high rents inflicted on the peasants increased as its service to the poor declined. By the middle of the 16th century, the Church owned half of Scotland's wealth and Monarchical support, which suited the King, but not the noblemen. These great families opposed both Crown and Church in the fight with the Reformation party, to which, unlike most of the European upper classes, it gave support. There *was* some merit on the spiritual side of the Church, if little on the secular. It established eight religious houses of Dominican and teaching Friars, along with Carthusians, Grey Friars and Augustinians. There were Mendicant Orders with no desire for property for the fineries of the secular priesthood. They worked in their gardens, cared for the poor, and tended the sick, especially the lepers. Perhaps, more important for the future, the monasteries encouraged learning – though not of the questioning sort, created the first libraries in Scotland, and started three universities for the training of priests. These in the fullness of time were used to train pastors for the Presbyterian Church the world over.

There were few priests and fewer places of worship. The priests' knowledge of Christianity was basic; some would have spoken Latin and could read the Bible; but they were the barrier between God and the people. The Mass and the serving of the Mass was for the priest *not* the people, as it had been since 323 AD when the Emperor Constantine chose the Church of Christ and Paul as the official religion of the Roman Empire. The Presbyterian Church brought God, the priest and the people together, probably for the first time since Paul. Life was governed by a perpetual fight with semi starvation, poor health, in a country riven by senseless violence, with no correcting instruction from either Church or gentry. Life was, in fact, lax, brutal and short. And insofar as the gentry concerned itself with the Church, it was to gain preferment and the benefice that went with it for the more stupid of their sons.

The Cathars of the Albigensian Heresy in French Languedoc, the 12th century Waldensians of Lyons, the Manichaeans and Gnostics of the 2nd century; all of whom had one common trait, they believe man could speak directly to God without priestly intervention. This was anathema to the Papacy and could not be, and was not, tolerated, leading to savage retribution.

On the fringes of Christianity, Scotland escaped the religious ferments in Europe that were the bane of Rome. Yet it was this pious desire that was one of the driving forces that established the Presbyterian Church worldwide and set it apart from England and Continental ruptures with Rome.

The middle of the 16th century found the Church in Scotland in a lamentable state. The corruption and abuses of every sort which dominated public and private life was worse than in England, no paragon of virtue. Granting ecclesiastical benefices to laymen reached the nadir of corruption, or the heights of absurdity, whichever way you care to regard it, when a child before it would walk was granted a preferment. Avarice, venality and luxurious living among the higher ranks of the clergy were endlessly on show. Everything that Martin Luther thundered against and triggered his break with Rome in 1512. The ordinary people always suffered most from the misdeeds of the secular Church.

The Beggars' Summons

On New Year's Day 1559, a remarkable document was found nailed on the gates of every religious building in Scotland. Author unknown, but written in the language of a scholar, its complaint was that of a poor man. It began by naming those for whom and to whom it spoke. "The blind, crooked, lame, widows, orphans, and all other poor visited by the hand of God as may not work, to the flocks of all friars within this realm we wish restitution of wrongs past, and reformation in times coming." The document ends with an inflammatory threat.

"Wherefore, seeing our number is so great, so indigent, and so heavily oppressed by your false means that none taketh care of our misery, and that it is better to provide for these our impotent members which God hath given us, to oppose to you in plain controversy than to see you hereafter, as you have done before, steal from us our lodging, and ourselves in the mean time to perish, and die for want of the same; we have thought good, therefore, ere we enter into conflict with you to warn you in the name of the great God by this public writing affixed on your gates where ye now dwell that ye remove forth of our said hospitals, betwixt this and the feast of Whit-Sunday next, so that we the lawful proprietors thereof may enter thereto, and afterward enjoy the commodities of the Church which ye have heretofore wrongfully holden from us: certifying you if ye fail, we will at the said term, in whole number and with the help of God and assistance of his saints on earth, of whose ready support we doubt not, enter and take possession of our said patrimony, and eject you utterly forth of the same. Let him, therefore, that before hath stolen, steal no more; but rather let him work with his hands that he may be helpful to the poor. "

This was the equivalent of Martin Luther's 95 theses on indulgences, denying to the Pope all rights to forgive sins, which were nailed to the Saxony church of Wittenburg. Within little more than 2 years Scotland made its own Reformation. The fastest change from Roman Catholicism to Protestantism in Europe, with no Counter Reformation nor its Thirty Years War.

Politics now entered into the contest for the soul of the Scots. James V (1513-42) wanting to improve the lot of the poor, sought advice from his English uncle, Henry VIII. Henry, having just broken with Rome, stripped the Church of its wealth and created the Church of England with himself as its Head. Henry advised him to do the same. That is, take the Church's wealth. This he was loathe to do, but the Rubicon was already crossed. As James was dying he received news of the birth of his heir, a daughter (who was to become Mary Queen of Scots). The fight was on, and in the 25 years before Mary, an unreconstructed Catholic, fled to England and her subsequent beheading by her cousin, Queen Elizabeth of England, she was briefly Queen of France, widowed, returned to Scotland, married Darnley (who was murdered), married Bothwell, Darnley's murderer, then abdicated in favour of her infant son by Darnley, James VI of Scotland, the heir to the childless Elizabeth and thus James I of England and the creator of the Ulster Plantation.

The Scottish nobility, always a thorn in the side of the Monarch, was the hammer that mortally wounded Roman Catholicism, mainly by getting rid of the French army, which had been resident in and around Edinburgh for too long. This, to the great benefit of the people, opened the door to John Knox, from Switzerland by way of Geneva, and his friend and mentor, Calvin. Knox put the pieces of the New Church together and it was called the Presbyterian Kirk. What matter that the nobility and gentry, driven partly by greed were the inheritors of the Church's great wealth, rather than the Crown? Politics had come to the aid of religion.

Scotland, having got rid of the French influence, which had been the bulwark of Catholicism there, began to see merit in England despite the centuries of war and devastation. The "auld enemy" had at least first opened the people's eyes to Protestantism. Knox had much in common with John the Baptist. Both swept onto their religious stages like a *deus ex machina*. Henceforth under the pitiless guidance of Knox – an Old Testament Prophet in all but name, to whom the Pope was the Devil incarnate and Rome the repository of evil – the people responded to his tongue lashings and threats of hell fire, because he was seen to be an honest man, and on their side.

Religion took on a completely different meaning. They were taught that man should regulate his worship under the guidance of his pastor, elected by the elders of his Kirk, and not by a corrupt Church run from Rome. Belief in God, the teachings of Christ and his Resurrection, the certainty of life after death and a warm welcome in Heaven provided the Ten Commandments were kept without question. On the other hand, unlike the Church of Rome, who never failed to reassure the poor that their reward would be in Heaven, the Protestant faith with its high regard for hard work, honesty and thrift would also provide reward on earth, and with the Kirk's blessing. Such devotion, faith and duty built up a character that would be to the benefit of Scotland, Ulster and ultimately America in the centuries that lay ahead.

The *eminence gris* of Catholicism was Cardinal Beaton. Aristocrat, Francophile, he spent some time in 1519 at the French Court and was appointed Bishop of Mirepoix in 1537, not for devotion or belief in the Holy Scriptures but for politics – Scottish-French religious politics. A year later he received the Cardinal's hat, the Bishopric of Arbroath and a seat in the Scottish Parliament. A scourge of the Reformation, a bitter enemy of Protestant heretics, he was assassinated in 1546, perhaps justly so, having caused by burning at the stake the death of many Protestants. Not only evil, he was dissolute; his mistress, Marion Ogilvy, bore him three children.

Knox, passionate, devout but remorseless reformer was just the leader for a Protestant Reformation, Scottish style. Himself an ordained priest, had fought the influence of Beaton vigorously, but fell foul of the French at the Scottish Court and spent 18 months in the French galleys. Later he fled to England, Germany and finally Geneva, where he came under the influence of Calvin. He seems to have been back in Scotland more or less permanently from 1558 until his death in 1572. In his short life of 59 years, his influence in bringing Scotland to Protestantism is beyond price. For feminists of the 20th century, however, he may be best remembered as a hate figure, who wrote the pamphlet entitled "First Blast of the Trumpet against the Monstrous Regiment of Women."

Knox was the archetypal religious reformer, dominated by the one transcendent idea, indifferent to everything that did not contribute to its realisation. In argument he took no prisoners, and regarded the Pope as the Anti-Christ, while Reform was the will of God. An English Protestant said of Knox, that in one hour he could by his voice alone put more life into his hearers than the sound of 500 trumpets in their ears. There was not his equal until John Wesley, throughout much of the 18th century, brought Methodism to the people of England and America. Not infrequently 10,000 to 30,000 people were prepared to wait patiently for him to preach. He also had been an ordained clergyman as Knox was a priest, and like Knox he despaired of his Church, the Anglican Church, as it lost the respect of the poor.

When Parliament ordered its Ministers to draw up a Confession of Faith, Protestantism was home and dry, never again in danger.

Parliament, meeting on July 10th, put an end to the Church of Rome, as the State Church of Scotland. In a single day it passed three Acts; the first expelling the Pope, the second condemning all doctrines and practices contrary to those of the Protestant Faith, and the third forbidding the celebration of the Mass. Parliament also instructed the Ministers of the New Church to draw up a Confession of Faith; a statement of the Doctrines in which members of the New Church were to believe. Then the Ministers prepared the First Book of Discipline for the government of the Church, the Presbyterian Church which became the established Kirk of Scotland.

Mary, still only 19, ascended to the throne in 1561, to be faced by widespread Protestant triumphalism. The ensuing fight between Crown and Kirk was largely a struggle between Mary and Knox, marked by pathos of her impossible position, a political battle that could not be won, and Knox's rough tongue. The fight was lost, and Mary fled to her unhappy fate at the hands of her English cousin and the executioner's clumsy axe on February 1st 1587.

The Scottish Reformation was quite different to that in England 30 years earlier. The English Reformation was imposed from the top by Henry VIII with a brutal finality, brushing aside the opposition of the Bishops and Archbishops, either with axe or argument. The people were not involved. In Scotland it was the groundswell from the people that toppled the Crown and Catholicism. Some wit said that Scotland had moved from barbarism to civilisation in barely a generation. The achievements of the Kirk and its dedicated pastors over the next century were awesome; in a country with no art, no literature, and no architecture, it inspired the respect of the people and gave them a hunger for education.

The effect of Knox on the laity was similar to that of an Old Testament prophet; it was Pharisaical in the better and non-Christian sense of the word. The Ten Commandments were dominant. It was by them, along with morality and education, that the people were to live, an easy-going people, much given to a strong drink, and with no more than a nodding acquaintance with such matters as the sanctity of marriage. The Kirk succeeded so well that in no time at all, most of Scotland became intensely puritanical and bigoted, character traits that were like a second skin and accompanied the Lowland Scot almost everywhere. Their harshness in this new Puritanism was born out of hard life, bad landlords, poor food and many battles for centuries; and, after Knox, the terrible wars of the 17th century. Neither did they have the advantage of at least a veneer of education, books, and, for the times, a gentler way of life, like some of the English. Knox was a good student of Calvin, and probably a better leader. When the 20th century English novelist, P. G. Wodehouse wrote "You could never mistake a Scotsman for a ray of sunshine," he wrote, only half in jest.

What influenced the people most were the honesty, the unquestioning religious belief and the commitment of the pastors to them. This tempered the narrow-minded bigotry. The parishioner and pastor were one. They lived together, worshipped together, sometimes worked together, and for the first time, the Church seemed to be on their side. The contrast with Catholicism was a revelation. No Mass to separate the priest from the people, no idolatry in the church, no ostentation in the upper-strata of priests and Bishops, no executions for heresy. Many of the noble families hated the Catholic Church though for other reasons, and were swift to join the peasantry. No doubt there were elements of self-preservation in their change of heart; but no matter, it greatly strengthened the Kirk. This also was different to the events in England where the nobility was less inclined to abandon their Catholic faith. By the end of the eighteenth century, the Presbyterian Church of Scotland, along with its presence in Ulster and America, must have been the strongest Protestant force in Christendom.

The absence of books and education in the early days was replaced by sermons, the discourse from the pulpit. They were always long, very long, and would be talked and argued about from one Sabbath to the next. This was new, for the remoteness of the priest previously had inhibited discussion. The people felt a dignity that had been lacking; and the ministers visited the sick, succoured and comforted the dying. To this the people responded warmly. Of course, after the sermon, the pastor would name and shame those guilty of drunkenness, fornication and, worst of all, breaking the Sabbath. When, previously in recorded history, had a clergy so stirred an illiterate people that its latent intellect awoke to become a massive component in a new, inclusive faith?

Protestantism became a force for good, throughout the land, mentor and master leading the community from the Kirk, in worship, work and social activities, guiding the people in their relationship to God and each other. Once a year, the Kirk brought together everybody, men and women, from all regions and classes, rich and poor. They met in the General Assembly. There, they discussed the welfare, and organisation of the Kirk, which was self-governing, and each region's Presbytery. Both General Assembly and Presbytery were an early form of democracy where the voice of the most lowly could be heard along with those of the great and the good. In a relatively short time the Kirk sought to achieve two fundamental reforms; the creation of nationwide literacy so that the clergy would be well educated and the people able to seek out the Word of God for themselves; and a transformation of the people's moral conduct.

If Knox and his fellow workers set out to make a perfect world out of an imperfect one, it failed in one area, an area not neglected in the rest of the world, itself far from perfect.: tolerance. Any element in a person's character, which seemed to thrive more strongly among non-believers than believers, received short shrift with Presbyterians. Intolerance gave strength to the Calvinist backbone, and Calvinism was not kind to sinners or heretics, though they did not wish to burn them. To the Scot, intolerance was the virtue that put them above others; that made them a chosen people that would not allow them to tolerate the presence of those who, in religious matters, chose to worship in another way. To them music, the theatre, art were not just frivolous but the Devil's invention and a short cut to Hell. The Catholic liturgy, the ritual of the Mass with its "smells and bells", the temptation of the Anti-Christ. Worship of God could never be beautiful only awesome and unquestioning.

Much of the rest of Europe, at the time Scotland was being converted, was in perpetual ferment; bigotry of every description divided one Christian sect from another. No one sect would accept the beliefs, liturgy or form of worship of the others, and the disagreements often took the form of killing heretics at the stake, broken on the wheel or the gallows. At least in Scotland heretics were only imprisoned. Only in the matter of witches did they conform with the rest of Europe: everybody burned witches and the Scots had just as much enthusiasm. The practice spread to America where nineteen innocent women were hanged at Salem in 1692.

It was a pity, also, that Luther's rage, which led to the Enlightenment of Calvin and others, did not arrive in Scotland along with the New Learning of science and philosophy, which the questioning minds of the Protestants swallowed hungrily.

The New Learning was anathema to Rome, considering it to be an attack on all they held holy. Rome believed that the study of natural science began and ended with Aristotle (288-322 BC), but Aristotle did not practice empirical science – the time had not been ripe for that. So for nearly 2000 years the Church had no interest in any science that seemed to deny Aristotle. In 1530 Copernicus proved the earth went round the sun, and not the reverse. Galileo proved the same 100 years later, but under pressure from the Inquisition, was forced to recant. The Church's refusal to allow scientific disclosures that went against the Church's beliefs held back industrial and social development in Europe for nearly 200 years. But not in England where the Reformation triggered the development of scientific philosophy and thus the Industrial Revolution. Scotland, when it tried to overcome illiteracy in the early 18th century, caught up. That, along with the discipline of the Kirk, made them admirable immigrants, and a powerful force for good in Ulster and, ultimately, in America.

3. A First Chronology

About 3000 BC The earliest known occupiers of Ireland. Probably hunter/gatherers succeeded by makers of tools and builders of habitations.

About 800-700 BC Arrival of the Celts from Eastern Europe. They were the most ancient Indo-European survivors in the West. The Celtic languages, of which Welsh is the most active modern survivor, once spread right across Europe. The best known Celt, though several hundred years after the first to arrive in Ireland, was St Patrick, captured probably in Wales by Irish Celtic raiders in the 4th century.

Christian era

1596 Hugh O'Neill, Earl of Tyrone, corresponded with King Philip of Spain, and bought guns and muskets to fight the English in a cleverly planned battle on the Ulster border. The first and only defeat of the English in 400 years of Anglo Irish Catholic warfare. The arithmetic was impressive; out of perhaps 4000, the English lost 2000 dead and 1000 wounded. Artillery and suppliers losses were considerable. It was a moral as well as a physical victory.

1607 The Flight of the Earls. Hugh O'Neill, Earl of Tyrone, continued guerrilla warfare against the English, causing death, starvation and destruction over most of Ireland. Finally, deciding that this way of life for the last 400 years was over, he decided to leave. So, along with some 100 followers, women, children, priests and bards, the Earls of Tyrone and Tyrconnel embarked quietly on a boat, sailing to Continental Europe, never to return. With the departure of the greatest Gaelic leader, the Gaelic order that had lasted for 2000 years came to an end. Descendents can be found all over Europe. One of them Graf (Earl) von Tyrconnel, an officer in the German army, was killed fighting against the Russians in 1942. The departure left the Catholic Irish effectively leaderless.

1610 This is the date generally given for the Plantation of Ulster. Presbyterian Scots from the Lowlands of Scotland started to move over the water. In fact, realistically it began in 1606, organised by private citizens and companies. After the Flight of the Earls in 1607 their lands reverted to the Crown, probably illegally, but James I had his way and he had 3,000,000 acres at his disposal. By 1620 an estimated 50,000 Scots and not a few English established themselves in Ulster.

1636 A group of clergymen with a fair group of their congregations set out for New England but were turned back by violent storms.

1640 100,000 Scots (and some English) now in Ulster.

1641 The Catholic Irish in rebellion against the Ulster Protestants. Greatly outnumbered, some 10,000 Protestants are slaughtered, and this date is seminal in the psyche of the Protestants, even into the present day. The rebellion lasted until 1650, when Cromwell the Puritan, came over with his English army, and was strictly fair in establishing peace. He killed both Catholics and Presbyterians alike.

1663 The Staple Act. This prohibited the direct exportation from Ireland of anything except horses, provisions and indentured servants. It was another stone in the shoe, another irritant to the Ulster people.

1684 A steady movement of small groups from the Presbytery of Laggan near Belfast went to America. There were now more than 500,000 Scots in Ulster.

1685 The Edict of Nante was revoked by France. Since enacted by Henry IV it had for nearly 100 years protected the Calvinist Huguenots from Catholic persecution. Of the more than 500,000 that fled France, many came to England, and not a few to Ulster with King William's approval. They brought skills and crafts of a high order to the benefit of their protectors: and their contribution to Ulster was to the improvement of manufacturing processes in the linen industry for which the colony was already noted. Of the many waves of immigrants to England through history that of the Huguenots was probably the most beneficial. America also gained as many settled in the Carolinas and New York.

1689 The Siege of Londonderry. Untrained men held out for

105 days against a large French army. Many dead and wounded from artillery fire.

1690 Battle of the River Boyne. King William, successor to the deposed James II, with a polyglot army including many Ulstermen, defeated the Continental army of James, which included 25,000 Irish Catholics. The date was July 12th, which is celebrated vigorously every year in Northern Ireland.

1699 The Woollens Act. A crippling blow to Ulster trade.

1703 The Test Act was passed by Queen Anne. This required all office holders in Ireland (magistrates etc) to take the sacrament of the Established Church *i.e.* Church of England. The Presbyterians considered this to be an attack on freedom of worship. It was hardly that, since Scotland had appointed Presbyterianism as the state religion, and such practice was normal throughout Europe. Nonetheless it was another black mark against the English, to hasten departure for America.

1714-19 Six years of an unusual mixture of rain and drought gave almost famine conditions, and farmers were in despair. Tiny grain and vegetable crops made food expensive, and poor flax crops all but ruined the linen industry. Tight rations and heavy unemployment, added to the other disturbing factors, made for an angry and dissatisfied people. A new life in America beckoned – not for the first time – and the more adventurous started to take stock. But the greatest incentive of all to emigration was to escape the injustice of rack renting.

1717-20 The First Wave. Five thousand sailed West in 1717. 55 ships sailed to America.

1725-29 The Second Wave. This departure contained so many people that the English Parliament in London appointed a commission to investigate the causes of departure as it seemed to portend the loss of the entire Protestant element of Ulster.

1729-50 The Third Wave. During this period a famine in 1740-41 caused the death of 400,000. This was a magnitude of disaster only otherwise encountered in the potato famine of 1846-48.

There is no doubt that this catastrophe hastened the third wave of departure. Arthur Young, the English economist, estimated that in this period Ulster lost a quarter of her trading cash and probably a quarter of its population engaged in manufacture.

1775 In the 58 years, since the commencement of substantial emigration, in excess of 200,000 Ulster folk, Protestant people, mostly of the Presbyterian faith, arrived in America.

4. Escape from Scotland

Who were these people – the Scotch Irish? Sometimes perhaps in mild perplexity called "The People with no Name." The English had never used the term; the Americans have always used it. Perhaps because they brought with them that dissenting arm of Christianity, Presbyterianism, and that, as every Anglo-American knew, grew out of the harsh austere soil of Scotland. Earlier they could just as well have called some of the Pilgrim Fathers Anglo Cornish, as they came from Cornwall in the South West of England, a former Celtic territory, where even now a proportion of the current population calls for an independent State. Their forebears came from Brittany in Western France, who also from time to time want to be separate from France.

To many, perhaps in ignorance, "Ulstermen" would have been more logical. For that was the ancient province from which they came: and the Presbyterians in Ulster had mostly been there 100 years or more before voting with their feet, by taking ship to America. Today, for those bearing the burden of gender sensitivity "Ulster Folk" could be a clear and splendid name. The word "Irish" is often believed to refer to someone who is a Roman Catholic, and whose ancestors arrived in America more dead than alive in the 1850s and 1860s, survivors of the potato famines which killed over a million. The Ulster Protestant Irish of course had preceded them by 150 years, were already running much of America, and had Produced four or five Presidents, to be followed by many more of Ulster Protestant ancestry.

In the sixth and seventh centuries AD the Lombards came over the Eastern Alps to live in the North of Italy centred on Pavia. But to call a citizen of Milan or Turin a Lombard today would be to receive a look of incomprehension. In the same way a Frenchman in Normandy France would be surprised to be called a Norseman of Norway, who moved into north west France at about the same time as the Celts were conquering Ireland. So why were those vigorous, bad tempered, argumentative, freedom-loving people who, starting with a trickle, flooded into the State of Pennsylvania between 1710 and 1760 – plus many more later – not just called Ulstermen; or even just Irish? Does it matter? It certainly does. Call them what you will, nobody doubts that from colonial times, they were considered, after a shaky start in Pennsylvania, a people of superior virtues, who could claim with justice to have contributed more to American constitutional liberty than most other immigrant peoples. Above all things, they wanted to be considered as, just "Americans."

Their Scottish origins were always freely discussed because they carried not as a burden, but rather as a badge of pride their rampant, aggressive Protestantism, well honed on the teachings of Knox and Calvin, and which they were prepared to defend in argument or battle. Such beliefs to them were above nation, above patriotism, they belonged to God. Even Knox was not above suspicion, as he never absolutely freed himself from the Episcopalian stranglehold of the established Church of England. Nobody hated bishops like the Ulster Protestants who considered them all to be tainted by Popery.

Their reasons for migrating were many, but only modestly included religious persecution, unlike the Germans who suffered fearful persecution on religious grounds from the Roman Catholic Church. Neither did they include severe political or industrial hardships, bad as they were from time to time. Indeed they were not slow to proclaim they expected to enjoy the freedom and liberty of the individual, expected by any subject of the English Crown, to which they were strongly and touchingly loyal. Just as today the Protestant Ulster people are the most loyal subjects of Queen Elizabeth, more so than the English.

To understand the Scotch Irish character, something of their origins and background must be known before, complete with families, they quitted the Scottish Lowlands at the time of the 1610 Plantation in Ulster. They were quite different to the Gaelic speaking Highland Scots, who were the poorest of the poor in a desperately poor land. The Highlanders were in attitude and mindset more akin to the Catholic Irish, with whom they shared both religion and language, and resisted with their lives the blandishments of the Protestant Reformation. Fighting two bloody wars, the 1715 and the 1745 against the English and Lowland Scots, in which they won a technical victory in the 1715 rebellion (for that is how the English described it), and vanquished in the 1745. After the latter, which was short but bloody, they were treated with great cruelty well after the battle was over. Even so, the survivors, those who were unable to flee to Catholic Spain or France, never lost their Catholic faith in what was by then a strongly Protestant Presbyterian Scotland.

The Lowlands, contained roughly that area south of a line running south west from Edinburgh to the Firth of Clyde, were inhospitable; thin soil and few trees as substantial forests had been felled for fuel and other purposes. In the west the climate was wet and cold giving meagre crops; in contrast the east, bordered by the North Sea, was fertile and gave a slightly higher standard of living. However, the whole of the Lowlands suffered a lower standard of living than that of the peasantry of England. It was, in short, a good place to leave if the opportunity to do so ever came.

King James VI of Scotland since infancy, son of the beheaded Mary Queen of Scots, succeeded Queen Elizabeth of England on her death in 1603 as King James I, and united the two countries. As what appeared to be an act of great statesmanship, he encouraged landowners and merchants of Scotland to go to Ulster, where they were granted huge areas of land. They in their turn encouraged their tenants to join them. At the same time, wealthy English were granted land in the other three provinces of Leinster, Munster and Connacht. This was not just generosity on the part of King James but enlightened self-interest. He, unlike his Catholic mother, was a Protestant, and the purpose of the Plantation was to establish a bulwark against Irish Roman Catholicism, and thus deter the French and their Spanish allies from attempting an invasion of England by way of Ireland. The plan worked.

The Pope in Rome refused to allow Henry VIII to divorce Catherine of Aragon, his Spanish Queen. In a fit of pique he declared his creation of the Church of England and was ex-communicated for his pains. Later, so was Queen Elizabeth. Under ex-communication any Catholic was declared to be without sin should he kill a Protestant monarch of England. So any actions an English sovereign took in Ireland was governed by fear of a Catholic invasion from the continent of Europe. This must always be born in mind when considering the relationship between England and Ireland. To the English to be a Catholic was to be a potential traitor.

During the two thousand years in which the inhabitants changed from hunter/gatherers to a early civilization, there were regular population movements between the province of Ulster and

Scotland a mere handful of miles away. These movements would also have continued after the marauding Celts arrived about 800 AD; and on safety grounds for a long time after. No one can be sure when the twenty-mile causeway to Scotland vanished, but while it was there regular population movements would surely have happened. So when they returned, officially during the King James Plantation, it may have been like the Jews returning to Palestine after the Diaspora of 2000 years. Those Scots who, in the late 16th century, before the start of the Plantation could, with some justification, say they were as Scotch/Irish/Gaelic as any Southern Catholic Irish, with a similar blood line. The Ulsterman could, in fact, be considered to be as Irish as any Catholic. Moreover, before the movement across the Atlantic was in full flood, they had had four generations of assimilation and association with the Ulster Irish, which made them different from, though clearly related to, the Lowland Scots of the Mainland.

The reasons for the immigration of the Lowland Scots to Ulster are well established and understood: poor soil, bad weather, *ergo* poor crops, low standard of living unlikely to improve, at least. Such conditions were not rare in the Western world; but such a mass movement of people *was* rare unless caused by widespread war and destruction. Those who did move had something about them that set them apart from those who stayed. Restless, angry, dissatisfied with their lot, inclined to argue with the bosses; a touch of scalliwaggery perhaps. Honest? Well, yes, although later in America, someone uncharitably said of the Scotch Irish "They appropriated the Ten Commandments and anything else they could lay their hands on." A minister at Donagdee in the County of Down, wrote in 1645 "From Scotland came many and from England not a few, yet from all of them generally the scum of both nations who, from debt or breaking and fleeing from justice, or seeking shelter, come hither. Hoping to be without fear of man's justice, in a land where there was nothing." There was perhaps an element of truth in this. It takes all sorts to have the energy *and* the courage to up sticks and move into unknown and perhaps dangerous territory.

Consider a few historical parallels. The debtors shipped from London to Georgia in the 17th century: not criminals, but sent to a climate almost guaranteeing an early death at the hands of a terrible inhospitable climate, yet the survivors, few of whom returned home, were healthy and strong, and formed the bedrock of a vigorous adventurous people. The early miners in California, willing volunteers ready to take a chance in search of fortune, held in scorn by those, fearful of peril, who stayed at home. The "criminals" transported in the prison hulks by sea to Australia from 1788 to 1868 by English Law, to a barren, hot, disease-ridden country, peopled by a few Aboriginals. Those who survived the punishment of the 12-month voyage, women and child criminals as well as men, then survived the harsh punishments inflicted, hard labour and sometimes 1000 lashes from the cat-o-nine tails for insubordination, were people of extraordinary character and fortitude. Thus from such unpromising conditions was created the Australian. The man whom the German General Rommel, in the desert battles of World War II, described as the finest infantryman of any army in the world. The English failed to understand they were deporting many of the best, strongest and bravest of their citizens, which action in the fullness of time they would come to regret.

The very day we landed upon the Fatal Shore
The planters stood around us, full twenty score or more;
They ranked us up like horses, and sold us out of hand,
They chained us up to pull the plough upon Van Diemen's Land.
said a Convict Ballad of 1825

The Lowland Scots were not criminals, were not beaten, and the journey to Ulster short with little discomfort. But they *also* must have been unusual men and women; most of whom had previously not travelled more than 10 miles from their village, but were ready to venture into the unknown.

The land that met the eyes of the first settlers was neither impressive nor welcoming. Many must have despaired, and considered returning to Scotland, visible across the sea on a clear day. Mist, heavy rains and a pervading dampness coming from the marshes was said to cause a disease called "a flux," possibly dysentery. It caused quite a few deaths, especially among English settlers from the London area, less hardy than the Scots, who came from a harsher background. It is sometimes forgotten that thousands of English were also part of the Plantation, and part of the flight to America. Perhaps "flight" is not the right word; "dignified exit" is much better. Land was plentiful. With the "Flight of the Earls", the Earls of Tyrconnel and Tyrone refugees in France and other places, in 1607, millions of acres were available in Ulster at the disposal of the Crown, with which to reward loyal subjects. In practice this meant giving to wealthy landowners in Scotland and England who rented the land to the settlers. The King giveth and the King taketh away. Blessed is the name of the King.

There were many complicated and infamous transactions, particularly in the counties of Down and Antrim where land moved into a new ownership through a persuasive piece of blackmail and connivance in high places. The victim Con O'Neill, nephew of the Earl of Tyrone, was locked up in Carrickfergus Castle on treason charges; he held title to 60,000 acres. Two devious Scottish businessmen, James Hamilton and Hugh Montgomery, promised O'Neill they could get him a royal pardon if he would pass 40,000 acres to them. O'Neill assented; sensibly deciding the loss of land was a distinct improvement on hanging, drawing and quartering, the punishment normally given to traitors. Hamilton and Montgomery later had no difficulty in stealing the remaining 20,000 acres. Rogues they may have been, but they were good developers, and transformed derelict wasteland into models of contemporary agriculture populated by Lowland Scots. Villages and churches were built and occupied with commendable speed, neat houses were plentiful, and one of the villages became the great city of Belfast.

For reasons not yet hardly touched upon, Ulster thus became a gathering point lasting 100 years or more from which started the huge, voluntary and unimpeded migration across the Atlantic to form what was to become perhaps the most cohesive and adventurous of peoples. So many races from so many nations but none greater than the Ulster Folk. They, along with the others, English, Scots, German, Dutch, Polish, Italian and Jews from everywhere who, in the fullness of time, were to become the greatest democracy in the world. Yet vast numbers of Americans still ask "Who are the Scotch Irish?"

It will always be difficult to describe with a single word a people of such complicated background. But let us not resort to considering as just "Irish" and include them in that dismissive, if humorous, epigram of the English "The Irishman was not born, he emerged from the primeval slime, fully grown and roaring drunk."

They are *not* nor should they be a people with no name.

5. The Province of Ulster: How the Scots Took Root

There were two movements towards settlement: a minor and a major. The minor was launched by English entrepreneurs such as Sir Arthur Chichester, the Lord Deputy in Dublin and the merchants of the London Guilds. These were an interesting group of Companies, peculiar English in character, all dating way back in history. They could best be described as early trade unions, and undoubtedly were formed to protect the working interests and jobs of their members. They basked, all twelve of them, in names that described their trade; Mercers, Grocers, Drapers, Fishmongers, Goldsmiths, Skinners, Clothworks, Merchant Tailors, Haberdashers, Salters, Ironmongers and Vintners. That is how they started, simple workers; how they finished up, the tradesman's skills lost in the mists of time was as the rules of the financial City of London; aldermen, very wealthy, from whom yearly the Lord Mayor of London was, and still is, chosen. Only one Lord Mayor is ever remembered, Dick Whittington (and of course his cat)! A mercer's apprentice, he became Lord Mayor in 1397.

As the financial centre of the world long before the Plantation, and at least until 1939, the London Merchants were quick to see Ulster as a good investment. The major movement was that of the Lowland Scots, and was central to the plan of James I, which was to establish by careful planning and investment to match, a colony loyal to the Crown, Protestant by religion, who would create towns and villages where none had existed before. Such colonization was by no means new in the world. The Greek city states of Alexander the Great, the Romans in the days of the Empire; and in the reign of Elizabeth, both Portugal and Spain had some success in the New World, but there was something about Ulster that was different. A combination perhaps of the climate, the character of the settlers and their success in dealing with adversity on a massive scale. The frontier spirit demonstrated in 18th and 19th century America was born in 17th century Ulster.

The English settlers were mainly small farmers from the Southern parts of England; ex-soldiers of good character, and they were offered fertile land at low rent on a long lease.

Beginning as a trickle in 1606, by 1620 at least 50,000 Lowland

Scots had crossed the 12 miles of water that divided Scotland from Ulster, to establish themselves in the wild, barren country, torn asunder by the wars between the Irish Earls and the English before the Earls left for France. An ill-clad, mostly barefoot, savage, sullen people, speaking a strange Gaelic dialect, met them. Living in rough cabins or caves, outnumbering them by perhaps 8 to 1, probably the poorest people in Europe, and certainly the poorest in the British Isles. They had been forbidden their Catholic Faith; their natural leaders had fled, leaving them to a handful of priests, almost as illiterate as their flocks and just as poor.

It must have been a sight both daunting and frightening. Many must have wondered if they had made a horrible mistake. But at least two-thirds of the land was theirs: cheap and on long leases. The Irish were (for the present) allowed to keep the rest, which was poor with much bog and mountain; and they clung relentlessly to their Faith, despite much persecution by the English yet to come.

The Scotch newcomers were largely practising Presbyterians; who considered Anglicanism almost as objectionable as Catholicism, and with good reason. The great landowners on the other hand were wealthy Anglicans ennobled because of their great land holdings; as firm in their religious beliefs as any Presbyterian or Catholic, but in the manner of English pragmatism, they were inclined to "live and let live" in the interest of successful business and communities. The feudal system they had left behind them in much of Scotland was to continue for the best part of another century. But feudalism did not transplant to Ulster, and the relationship between landlord and tenant was a far cry from that of master and serf.

The Province of Ulster consisted of Donegal, Derry (changed to Londonderry), Tyrone, Fermanagh, Cavan, Monaghan, Antrim, Armagh and Down. Private planters were already at work in Antrim, Down and Monaghan. About 500,000 acres of decent land, though including a fair amount of bog and forest, were available to the Scotch settlers in the other six counties.

James I was as canny a Scot as any of his countrymen who made their fame and fortune throughout the world and across the centuries. He was determined that Ireland should no longer be the drain on England's Exchequer in his reign as it had been in the time of Elizabeth. One of his most brilliant schemes to raise ready cash

The Frontier Spirit

As the British soldiers at the battle of Mons on 27th August 1914, sorely pressed by the German First Army, claim they were saved and encouraged by a vision in the sky of the English long bowmen at Crecy, where in 1346 the English defeated the French; so some of the men at the Alamo in 1836, as they fought and died gallantly against impossible odds, may have remembered the siege of Londonderry in 1689, where their ancestors repulsed a large French force successfully for 105 days. 15 of the 183 who fell at the Alamo mission house were Ulstermen and 12 were English.

was started in 1611. He created the new Order of Baronet, a rank of nobility between a Baron and a Knight, and the title was hereditary. A Baronet could bear the title of "Sir", solely on payment of £1,000 to the Crown; a huge amount at the time, but there was no shortage of would-be gentlemen in England, Scotland and Wales ready to fork out £1,000 for a Baronetcy, and the money would go towards the cost of maintaining soldiers in Ulster. He would also have the right to a coat of arms bearing the Bloody Hand of Ulster. In a very short time 205 English landowners put their hand into their pocket to give the Exchequer the handsome sum of £205,000.

A Presbyterian minister of the time commented:

"The King had a natural love to have Ireland planted with Scots as being, beside their loyalty, of a middle temper, between the English trader and the Irish rude breeding, and a great deal more like to venture to plant Ulster than the English, to lying far from both the English native land and more from their humour, while it lies nigh to Scotland. And the inhabitants not so far from the ancient Scots manner; so that it might be hoped that the Irish untoward living would be met both with equal firmness, if need be, and be especially allayed by the example of more civility and Protestant profession than in former times had been among them".

It was the King's intention to spread the allocation of land widely, a hedge betting operation. He wanted shrewd, experienced businessmen who knew how many beans made five, and could balance thrift with investment. He wanted landowning aristocrats, who understood man management and could inspire loyalty. He got both, especially from Galloway in the south-west of Scotland. The City of London moneymen were firm in his sights; he got them too. Thinkers and scholars were not neglected. In short, he got them all, and they would be his agents, working for the King and Crown. An Irish, or rather Ulster upper class was born. Not unlike perhaps the rulers of democratic Athens of Pericles in 500 BC but without the slaves. These were the Lords and gentry of Scotland and England; veterans of the Irish and European wars, the London City Guilds; the Established Church of Ireland, and Trinity College Dublin. Such notables, bent on building a colony worthy of God and Mammon, and a practical example of the Protestant work ethic, which in the fullness of time was to reach its apogee in America.

Half the allotted 250,000 acres for distribution was placed in the hands of "undertakers", who rented out substantial packages of land to "servitors". Any nobleman or gentleman in Scotland or England could apply for a grant and, on approval of his application, the undertaker would then agree to "plant" his new estate with Protestant tenant farmers from either of the two countries, and build on the estate a castle of sorts within a fortified enclosure called a "bawn". Servitors were to be Protestant ex-officers and soldiers, rewarded with land for loyal service to the Crown, and who would be doughty defenders in times of trouble. They were expected to build houses, and, in exceptional circumstances, take Irish tenants. All this in a Province that in two thousand years had never seen a stone house or fortification or any group of habitations that could remotely be called a village, much less a town. It could easily be described as an early exercise in social engineering, and, ironically in an age of absolute monarchy, when monarchs controlled their subjects absolutely.

Land dished out by the Scottish Undertakers was, in some ways, to create a special Ulster character. For those counties seeded mostly by Scots were largely the Presbyterian sect of Christianity, whereas other counties settled by the English were either Puritans or belonged to the Established Church of Ireland.

Donegal and Tyrone were entirely Scots occupied. Armagh and Derry (or Londonderry) were prevailingly English. Fermanagh and Cavan were mixed. The other 3 counties of the 9, which formed the ancient Province of Ulster, were not officially part of the Plantation but had been successfully settled. Down and Antrim were planted by the unscrupulous but clever Scots, Montgomery and Hamilton; and without them there may have been no Belfast, and no Shankill Road, the centre of Ulster Protestant hard men, and part of this book's title.

The Scottish part of the Plantation was controlled by the Privy Council in Edinburgh, and they made public the news inviting applications for land grants. By September 1610, 77 had applied. This number was reduced to 59, and by 1611 they had been allotted 81,000 acres. Of the 59, five were noblemen of title and the rest gentry. All were Lowlanders in the south-west, from whence they might see the shores of Ulster.

Physically settled they certainly became, but in the mind they must have been sorely troubled. They were never allowed to forget they had usurped the sullen Irish Catholics' land and birthrights. If people simmering with resentment of the poor hand of cards history had dealt them, yet greatly outnumbering the usurpers, whose descendants 100 years later when defending the Frontier in America must have remembered their forebears in Ulster. Yet once again they were the usurpers, and the Indians the dispossessed. What did Marx say about history "It repeats itself, first as tragedy, then   as farce"?

King James VI and I knew his people better than did his English courtiers: their adventurous nature, experience of desperate poverty, both of which made them eager to escape, and *who* could resist a good bargain? A lease of 21 years – maybe for life, on a good soil, to replace a short lease on poor soil in Scotland? No contest was declared on that one. The role of the undertaker was vital and his duties to some extent closely defined. For example, for an estate of 2000 acres he was expected to find 48 able-bodied men from Scotland or Ireland. He also had to grant land of specified areas to tenants, and also provide muskets and other weapons for the tenants for defence purposes if required.

Few of the schemes and enterprises moved smoothly in the early days. Murphy's Law, or perhaps McDuff's, provided a host of stumbling blocks. The Ulster Plantation was no different. On occasions, Undertakers promised much but delivered little. Others were idle and under-performed. The more ambitious could never get enough farmers, and in the case of some English, the harsh weather and working conditions were hard to stomach, and they moved back to England. The Scots were more accustomed to hard work and small reward. Many English remained and prospered, but the main body of settlers was always Scottish.

Despite severe instructions not to employ Irish labour was obeyed in the letter but not the spirit of the law, especially on the great estates. The prohibition was everywhere flouted, and attempts to enforce the Law vigorously opposed. Without the Irish peasant many estates would have been gravely undermanned, especially at harvest time. Many Irish, of course, found themselves employed on land formerly their own and for poor wages. In Scotland, particularly in the Highlands, the clan chieftain laird, squire, call him what you will, inspired respect. This was because the clan was held together by strong bonds of loyalty in order to survive. Hard living, short rations and fear of external attack encouraged mutual support. This strength of "all for one and one for all" travelled with the emigrants to Ulster and gave them the tenacity, and indeed, sheer bloody-mindedness not only to survive but to prosper. More good news than bad travelled back home, across the narrow waters and encouraged others to come.

Of all the land at the disposal of James, one tenth was made available to "natives of good will" ie. the Irish. This group was mainly Irish gentry with a pedigree stretching back to the Celts and the Normans, some 500 years. They were made poor through being on the wrong side in the Irish/English wars, not to mention the Irish/Irish wars. The Irish gentry naturally chose Irish peasants to work for them. It was *not* an over-generous gift. The size was small, no more than 25 acres and on poor land, and usually on a "for life" interest. They were not liked by the Protestants, and felt they were tolerated only out of necessity. The Plantation settlers probably feared them through guilt, and the Privy Council in Edinburgh were in grave error if they expected to win them over to a new state of affairs in Ulster.

The arrival of ministers of the Kirk from Scotland must have strengthened all, to combat and triumph over the many problems, many distressing events, put up by the move to the new land. Armed with the unyielding spirit of John Knox, it was like the arrival of a New Reformation, when the ministers came; and Scotland the land of their forefathers seemed closer to a new life in which there was hope of a better future.

The Plantation succeeded. Had it failed Northern Ireland would not now be British and both parts of the island would be united as one. There would have been no rebellion in 1798 and no civil war in 1922. No Protestant Ulster of the Six Counties, and no bloody conflict with the IRA. Of course, there would have been no great migration to America either, and thus no Scotch Irish to play such a formidable part in the Revolutionary War of 1776-81 and the Civil War of 1861-65.

Amazingly, this bulwark against Papistry survived the departures to America, and the Ulsterman everywhere displayed a new freedom to strike his own bargain; ready to decide his own future and that of his family. Ulster struck a blow for individualism and nowhere was it to be more apparent than in America.

6. The Other Irish Plantations

Munster

There were two attempts to establish an English Plantation in Munster, which unlike Ulster, protected by lakes, rivers and mountains and facing Scotland, lay in the South of Ireland, facing the direction from which the French and Spanish from time to time threatened invasion. It was the first English venture into genuine colonialism, predating the New England Settlements by 50 years. The preceding four centuries of English involvement in Irish Gaelic affairs were opportunistic and usually by invitation from one or other of the Gaelic Chieftains. Munster was different, planned, but badly planned, giving but scant regard to the difficulties that would inevitably face English settlers in a sequestrated land, where the people could be assumed to be hostile from the beginning. Everything was to end in chaos after bloody military engagements; conflicts with great cruelty inflicted by both sides.

Once upon a time there were two great, mad, irrational, frivolous and murderous Norman Irish noble men who owned hundreds of square miles in the ancient Provinces of Munster and Leinster. One was Gerald Fitzgerald, the 14th Earl of Desmond, aided by his loyal families of O'Sullivans, MacSheehys and McCarthys. The other was Thomas Butler, 10th Earl of Ormonde, with his cohorts of O'Kennedys, Burkes and MacGillipatrics. Both came to Ireland in about 1200 with King John of Magna Carta fame, and both were absolute Monarchs in all but name. They were intermarried at various levels, and their favourite pursuits were drinking, whoring and fighting each other. Cattle raiding was often the cause of conflict; and one such was of sufficient magnitude as to attract the attention of Queen Elizabeth of England. Three hundred Desmonds were killed and many wounded. The Queen, beside herself with rage, ordered both Earls, Desmond badly wounded, to London . A minor war, and for what? For cattle. Ormonde the Catholic, but in his own interests loyal to the Protestant English Crown, and brought up at the English Court, was admonished and pardoned. Desmond, a devout and unrepentant Catholic, was first imprisoned in the Tower for two years; then paroled to house arrest in a London friend's house. He was later entrapped on a false treason charge, and forced "voluntarily" to surrender the title to his lands and renounce his title to save his life. This was the excuse the Queen wanted to set up an English Plantation in Munster, with English armed settlers to repel any Continental fleet. It was a disaster.

The Queen wanted a candidate as leader to fit the job description of "a country gentleman, of adventurous disposition, experienced as a soldier who could put up a plausible claim to a land title in Munster." Enter Sir Peter Carew, West Country gentleman, accompanied by his lawyer Hooker (well named); well trained in turning spurious claims into copper-bottomed certainties. The Queen was satisfied, as was the Dublin Government. So in 1572 Carew successfully recruited like thinking landed gentlemen, prepared to go to Munster along with retainers, servants, ex-soldiers and farmers, including such famous names as Admiral Sir Richard Grenville, Sir Humphrey Gilbert, half brother of Sir Walter Raleigh, famous for bringing the potato and tobacco to England.

Carew, rough in tongue and temper, and of abysmal ignorance, thought the Irish peasant, who had had no respect for law since the Celts and did not think law was applicable to him, could be easily turned into an English peasant who had been subjected to a stern but fair legal system since Roman or Saxon times. Carew decided to settle the matter by evictions, property burning, crop destruction and other means of the tyrannical landlord. He had obtained ownership of a huge acreage of Desmond land. Throughout the Province the same cycle was followed. Eviction of the Irish by the English, distribution of land, construction of buildings, clearance and cultivation. Not the best policy for winning the hearts and minds. The peasants, skilled in guerrilla warfare and raids, reacted with their own brand of killing, burning and destruction. Many settlers were massacred, and English troops had to be shipped to Ireland to save what settlers they could. Famine descended on Munster, and an uneasy peace on a sullen people. It was a Pyrrhic victory; the English settlements were destroyed and the Queen decided, for the moment, to allow a return to the *status quo ante bellum*.

Desmond was allowed to return, his land restored, and he immediately exacted his own style of revenge; hanging any English officials he could find. The first Plantation was over and the soldiers remained to keep the peace or what passed for peace in Munster.

The second Munster Plantation started in 1578. Better planned, but even more bloody, more cruel than the first. The English had no choice but to keep a permanent army in Ireland, which was to remain there until 1922. But their strategic thinking was correct :many landings by the French and Spaniards were repulsed. The reasons for the Munster Plantation failure were best summed up by the poet Edmund Spencer, Clerk to the Munster Council, in his report to the Queen. "The deviser of the settlement of Munster perhaps thought that the civil example of the English being set before the Irish, and their daily conversing with them, would have brought them by dislike of their own savage life to the liking and embracing of better civility. But it is far otherwise, for instead of following them, they ignore the English, and most hatefully shun them, for two causes; first because they have ever been brought up licentiously, and to live as each other listeth; secondly, because they naturally hate the English, so that their fashions they also hate."

The same sentiments of rage and bewilderment were later echoed by colonizers the world over. The words could have been used by Americans (many of them Irish) about Indians; Australians (also with a large Irish component) about aborigines, and French colonialists about indigenous Algerians. Purveyors of what they consider to be better values are seldom popular with their audiences, and usually become arrogant and impatient.

Limerick: the Moravians

The history of Ireland does not yield too many success stories. Migrations and emigrations contained, at least in the early days, more horror than happiness. Surprisingly there is one immigration that almost from the beginning contained little else but success, a success brought about by the tenacity of the immigrants. The Holy Roman Empire created some strange anomalies; none more so than the Palatinates. These were areas, perhaps provinces, ruled by a Count of the Roman Catholic Church and thus with authority derived from Rome. There were several among the polyglot of German speaking states, and even one in England. There was a Protestant sect who came from Moravia, a province of the Austrian Empire south of Prague. Persecuted as a minority in a devout Catholic country, the Moravians migrated to various places, and many ended up in the Kingdom of Bavaria, also a Catholic country. A classic case of jumping out of the frying pan into the fire; and so it proved to be. Then their luck changed. During the War of the Spanish Succession (1701-13), the Duke of Marlborough, Winston Churchill's illustrious ancestor, humbled the French, allowing England once again to hold the balance of power in Europe. His greatest victory was at Blenheim in Bavaria in 1709, and the Moravians sought his protection, which he willingly granted; arranging for five thousand to settle in Ireland, in County Limerick. They were allotted eight- to ten-acre plots per family at a very small rent on a long lease. An industrious and closely-knit community, they brought skilled European farming practices, rather different to the haphazard methods of the Catholic Irish. When the leases came up for renewal in the 1760's the rents were raised from 5 to 30 shillings an acre. Some paid; others, still cohesive, moved south to County Kerry where land was cheaper.

Arthur Young, an English economist, visited the Limerick Moravians in 1776. He saw nothing but cleanliness in houses and barns, a prosperous people. They sowed wheat, barley, oats and potatoes in rotation; and also grew flax. Another visitor noted they still spoke German and raised animals for the table, while living on a diet of milk, potatoes, butter and bread. They were clearly a diligent, thrifty and hard working people. In due course this was to save their lives.

They also intermarried with Irish Protestants, of whom there were plenty among the Catholics, and were said to be ethnically intact after more than 130 years. Some said there was only one flaw in the intermarriage. Amidst all this prosperous efficiency of the Moravians, the Catholic peasants were much more cheerful and kindly, despite their poverty.

There is a dramatic postscript to this success story. During the great famine of 1741 and the even greater potato famines of 1848-50, none of the Moravian communities died of starvation. Why? Because they always practiced the rotation of many crops, and never the monoculture of the Catholic Irish, with their fatal reliance on the potato. The Irish suffered over one million dead in 1848-50 alone.

7. The Best of Times, The Worst of Times, and War

It took about 25 years before the colony could be said to be established. By then such land was already under the plough and in a state of stable cultivation that newcomers had some difficulty in finding suitable farms. There had been some fat years, and the native Irish were quiet, waiting their chance, it might be said. Increases in the number of settlers encouraged a feeling of security; safety in numbers; the presence of ministers of the church also gave a special sense of well being; if God is with us who can be against us? Who indeed? There *was* a long calm before the storm, but when it came it was of hurricane dimensions: killing, burning, destroying. God was even-handed and spared nobody. From 1634 onwards until 1690, the feeling of safety was at best irregular and the very existence of the colony was threatened. Similar troubles were endemic in Europe; Church and state were flexing their muscles against each other in the Thirty Years War, which was at least being fought in the name of Nationalism as much as for Religion.

The troubles were those that had always threatened newcomers in a hostile land. The natives *themselves* felt threatened; more particularly in Ireland where in the matters of religion and law, the government, England, favoured the newcomers. It was as though a virus, a disease, was spreading like a forest fire throughout Europe. Hardly a country was spared, certainly not Ireland.

Two men were then appointed who were to have a profound effect on the lives of the settlers. Thomas Wentworth, later Lord Strafford, became Lord Deputy of Ireland; and William Laud, later to become Archbishop of Canterbury. Wentworth had previously opposed the absolutist King Charles I, but had no sympathy with Puritans, and when their activities menaced the King, he became a Royalist. He was able, honest, wanting Ireland to prosper, but hostile to all sections of the people who opposed him: Irish, Irish English, Catholic or Protestant. An unusual man, while handing out severe punishments, he was at the same time helping the linen industry to develop by bringing in skilled labour from Holland, along with flax seed, at his own expense. He was determined that the Established Church of England would be the only religious voice in Ulster and

Ireland: the voice of Anglicanism. Typical of his penal laws was the "Black Oath" as it was called, which compelled all Ulster Scots over the age of 16 to swear loyalty to the King in every way, and to declare unlawful, the recent Scottish rebellion against the King's attempt to restore the bishops in Scotland. This so angered the settlers that many returned to Scotland, where the rebellion of the 1638 Covenant had successfully re-established Presbyterian practices, and ended once more the rule of the bishops, the servants of the Crown, and in the view of the Covenanters, the enemies of God.

Laud saw his duty as ensuring that High Church liturgy was established in all the King's dominions, by any means however harsh. It was his liturgy known as the Popish English Mass Book that caused the Scottish Rebellion of 1637 and thus the formation of the Scottish Covenant, which defeated him. All over Ireland he replaced Puritan bishops with his own, and pressured them to make Presbyterian ministers to conform with Church of England practices, including acceptance of the Thirty Nine Articles of the English Liturgy. This was a grievous blow, and for five years most Scottish Congregations in Ulster were without ministers. Secret sermons were delivered of course, and those who lived near the coast of Antrim would slip over the narrow sea to have their children baptised. It was during this time that one group lead by four deposed ministers tried to reach America but were turned back by violent storms and a craven ship's captain. Then, to use a modern idiom, it all went "pear shaped."

When the King planned his war of punishment in Scotland in 1640, Wentworth raised an army of Gaelic Irish to serve the King in Scotland. It totalled about 9000, but before it could embark, Wentworth was recalled by Charles to help him in his fight against Parliament, from which would emerge the only republic in the British Isles until Ireland, excluding Ulster, made the decision to leave the British Empire in 1922. Ironically, Wentworth had raised and trained a Catholic army of dissident Irish that before long would be used, not in Scotland but in Ulster, to massacre settlers.

Wentworth returned, and religious liberty was re-established, more or less, in Ulster by two Justices, one a Puritan Parliamentarian, and the other a sensible man aware of the damage done by Archbishop Laud. Many of those who had fled to Scotland returned to their farms; and a fresh wave of migration began only to be checked by the Irish Rebellion of 1641, which continued sporadically, with great cruelty and bloodshed on all sides, for eleven years. The Rebellion was a desperate act born of despair. Robbed of their ancestral lands, and almost denied the right to remain where they had lived for two thousand years, the Irish had seen the best land go to the usurpers; marshes drained, forest cut down, roads built, and for whom? Not for them; and *who* would not have risen to kill their enemies when the chance came, as it did?

An outsider now entered the game on the side of the Gaelic Irish, the Jesuit. Ignatius Loyola in 1534 formed the Society of Jesus, which was founded to combat Luther's Reformation and to propagate the Faith according to Rome through discipline, education and secrecy. It achieved such powers that it came in conflict with both religious *and* civil authorities in Rome. Not for nothing was its Vicar General known as the Black Pope. The Irish, leaderless since the "Flight of the Earls" in 1607, was a target for the Jesuits, and probably on instructions from Rome, came to Ireland to give guidance and spiritual aid, and to strengthen their hatred for Protestantism and other heretics. It was the Jesuits, skilled in secrecy and planning who taught the Irish how to keep details of the Uprising from the settlers, to whom it came as a surprise.

Rome was deeply involved, and it was Father Luke Waddington, English head of the Franciscan House in Rome, who had negotiated assistance, both from the Pope and Cardinal Richelieu, the most powerful political force in France. With such help it was inevitable that the Ulster Irish would show small mercy.

The English historian William Lecky summed up the mental resolve of the Irish when he wrote in 1892:

"Behind the people lay the maddening recollections of the wars of Elizabeth, when their parents had been starved by thousands to death, when unresisting peasants, when women, when children had been deliberately massacred, and when no quarter had been given to the prisoners. Before them lay the gloom and almost certain prospect of banishment from the land which remained to them, of the extirpation of the religion which was first becoming the passion as well as the consolation of their lives, of the sentence of death against any priest who dared to pray beside their bed of death."

The Woodkerns

The dispossessed, those with no land; perhaps no family and nothing to lose. Native Gaelic Irish known as "Woodkerns" were feared by the settlers, and operated in bands under the leadership of men who felt they had no choice but to live outside the law, or at least "Settlers' Law." The leaders were mostly impoverished Irish gentry, capable of putting together organised attacks, intelligent and merciless; living by plunder, they did at least offer some hope.

Ferocious laws were passed against them, and on capture were tried and hanged. Summary justice of the sort handed out by American colonialists in the 18th and 19th centuries to Indians who were foolish enough to defend themselves and their families against settlers hungry for land.

Sir Arthur Chichester, Lord Deputy in Dublin, and for the times a fair man, would neither pardon them nor allow them to leave the province unless they betrayed their leaders. Finally, he relented and allowed them to go to Sweden and enlist in the service of Gustavus Adolphus, the Protestant King of the North, against Spain and the Catholic allies in the Thirty Years War, which had been raging since 1618. The Irish hated this service, and deserted when they could to the Spanish so that they could at least fight with their co-religionists.

The Order of Battle was drawn. On the Rebels side the Gaelic Irish, the Old English Catholics and sundry Catholic help from Europe. On the other, the English Anglicans centred on Dublin, plus the Ulster settlers, mostly Presbyterians, along with English Puritans in the Southern provinces of Munster, Leinster and Connaught. The English garrisons in Ulster were overrun and the ghastly scenes of the destruction of the Munster Plantation settlements in 1578 were re-enacted in Ulster. Settlers and their families were slaughtered; stored crops were burned. The number of women and children killed was probably exaggerated, as that was the fashion of the times by contemporary propagandists. Certainly not the 200,000 dead, the number most favoured by Protestant sources. Neutral commentators, if such exist, think 15,000, still an enormous figure, the most likely. But it is the larger number that has entered the tenacious memory of Ulster Protestants. The English suffered worst, not only because the Irish held them responsible for most of their misery, but because they were at the forefront of the uprising. This gave the Scots a little time to prepare their defences. There was a statistician of the time, Sir William Petty, who calculated a population of 1,448,000 suffered a loss of 616,000 either by the sword, famine or plague; of this 504,000 were said to have been Irish. Once again, a serious historian will suspect these figures. After all, statistics is hardly an exact science even today. Of the survivors, many were deported to the West Indies, and thirty to forty thousand left Ireland to join the vast force of Irishmen fighting in European armies; on the Catholic side of course, or perhaps not: you could never be sure with the Irish.

Petty also said that before 1641, nationwide about two thirds of the good land was in Catholic hands, but by 1660 more than the same amount had passed into Protestant hands. The war caused marches and counter marches, the destruction of crops, the burning of houses and irregular warfare of a type peculiar to Ireland for centuries. One thing was certain, although most people were the losers, the poor lost the most, for they always do.

At this point Oliver Cromwell, the Lord Lieutenant and General for the Parliament of England made his personal intervention into Irish affairs. Brief and decisive, but it moulded the destiny of Ireland for 350 years. A man who, in his own country had won a civil war, cut off his King's head, disestablished the Church of England, outlawed the monarchy, and abolished the peerage, was unlikely to be unduly bothered by the problems to be faced in Ireland. He was a man who could reduce complex matters to simple ones. With most authoritarians the reverse is the case. He landed at Dublin on 15th August 1649, with 20,000 battle-hardened troops – soldiers, all subscribers to any number of religious sects, all untainted by Papistry. Fundamentalists to a man, making no bones about the Old Testament exhortations to exchange eyes for eyes and tooth for tooth, they were obsessed with their beliefs and the rectitude of what they were about to do. Unshakably convinced that all Irish Catholics must share the blame for the massacre of the Ulster Protestants in 1641, they were in Cromwell's eyes proper candidates for inflicting divine vengeance and the instrument appointed by Jehovah for this task.

Cromwell started out in life as a modest country gentleman, some land, quite well connected and not uncultured, but a Puritan of the mould of John Knox, who turned himself into one of the greatest generals in history. His first target for punishment was the medieval fortress town of Drogheda, 30 miles north of Dublin, and his planning was simple, logical and swift. The walls were pierced by artillery, the battlements stormed, the town entered and the people, men, women and children put to the sword. It was a textbook operation, even if it was a 12th century rather than a 17th century textbook. Estimates of the dead vary as always. Historians put it at 3,500 but the propagandist's once again prefer the figure of 30,000; it had a nice ring to it.

Drogheda was an unusual town, an Old English "Pale" town. The Pale was the name given to the part of Ireland where the English writ ran from the 12th century reign of Henry II and covered the counties of Louth, Meath, Kilkenny, Wexford, Waterford, Tipperary and Dublin. Its inhabitants and certainly its leading citizens must have been almost entirely English or of English descent and proudly so. How sadly ironical that Cromwell in his determination to take revenge should have chosen as victims a community whose forebears had ruled Ireland in England's name for 500 years. Cromwell got it wrong; he chose the wrong town. The horror of Drogheda was quickly followed by more of the same, and just as comprehensively at Wexford, a similar town to Drogheda, with an ancient royal charter. Sir Charles Coote, a Cromwell general, did the same bloody work in Ulster, and Lord Broghill in Munster. The pacification that had started in August 1649 was all but completed by March 1650. A military operation of surgical neatness, brilliant but bloody. The countryside was in ruins, and the population reduced by the sword, starvation and disease, to barely half a million. The final administrative details were completed with the efficiency expected of Cromwellian officers – and quickly. Thirty to forty thousand Irish soldiers were allowed to go to the armies of France and Spain, a good way to deal with a constant threat had they been allowed to stay. Surprisingly only fifty-two death sentences were handed out by the Dublin Court for complicity in the Ulster Massacre.

Arising out of Cromwell's campaign was what was known as the "Adventurers Act"; passed swiftly by the English Parliament which provides for the confiscation of Irish estates, to be sold subsequently to subscribers to be known as "Adventurers". Subscribers moved in quickly, but land was also given to Cromwellian soldiers: partly in lieu of pay but also to create a body of Protestants, trained ex-soldiers permanently resident in Ireland. The entire area of the country was put at twenty million acres, of which Cromwell's settlers took eleven millions. The exiled Catholics, mostly Old English, had 5 millions of poor quality land, mostly in the West. A predictable consequence was that soldiers who preferred cash sold their land and went home to England, and the buyers were shrewd ex-officers who greatly increased the size of their own land grants to very large estates. Puritans, like Presbyterians, were good businessmen. These *new* English landlords became an important element of that powerful sector of life in Ireland known as the Anglo-Irish, who were effectively to govern Ireland for the next 250 years, providing at the same time a large section of the officer caste in the British Army, Navy and later in the Royal Air Force – and, in a slightly disguised form, many, many officers in the American revolutionary army, and in the American Civil War on both sides.

Cromwell left Ireland in May 1650 never to return. The Lord Protector had tolerated no squabbles between Episcopalians and Presbyterians, and peace had been enforced by war. As Tacitus said of his Roman countrymen "They created a desert and called it peace."

Nevertheless, after the Ulster massacre of 1641, Cromwell *did* bring peace, and out of the desolation from 1650, Ulster *did* prosper, as also, though at a much lower rate, did the rest of Ireland.

Bad as the Ulster Settlers suffered in the war of 1641-50, the Gaelic Irish, and English, whether Puritans, Episcopalians or Catholics, almost certainly had many more dead and wounded. The number of Presbyterian ministers was down to seven in 1653; many must have returned to Scotland, but by 1660 there were seventy, serving 80 parishes with parishioners totalling 100,000. Not all were Presbyterians, but those who were not, were pleased to have the ministrations of a Protestant clergyman. With the monarchy restored in 1660, King Charles II was too occupied with matters closer to home, and Ulster and Ireland as a whole enjoyed a period of benign neglect from English interference. The first ten years of Charles' reign were good for Ulster. He showed admirable benevolence towards all the dissenting Protestant sects, in particular Presbyterianism. Religion was not of great concern to him, as long as it did not clash with his somewhat *louche* way of life; and religious persecution was rarely seen or discussed. The English element in Ulster also grew, and many must have ended up in America, with the Scotch Irish, who would perhaps have been surprised to find out they had more than a dash of English blood in their veins.

Population movements in Europe were many and for the usual reasons. Religious persecution was usually blamed, but there were others of which economics and a desire for a monarch to change his frontiers in relation to another, and in his favour. None was more important to England and Ulster, indeed to the whole of Ireland than the flight of the Huguenots from France. Persecution of the Huguenots was always an ongoing thing. The Catholic hierarchy hated them as heretics, for their cleverness and their liberal attitudes to science, philosophy and other pursuits, anathema to the Catholic Church. On St Bartholomew's Eve in 1572, fifty thousand Huguenots were killed all over France; twenty thousand in Paris alone. But in 1596 Henry of Navarre, a Protestant, was offered the Kingdom of France; at which he is said to have spoken the memorable and cynical phrase, "Paris vaut bien une messe" (Paris is worth a mass). Henry II succeeded in achieving a measure of toleration towards the Huguenots, which lasted for the best part of 100 years, by his Edict of Nantes, but in 1685, Louis IV revoked the Edict. The Huguenots, who were of course Calvinist, and remembering no doubt the St Bartholomew's Eve massacre, fled for their lives to those places where their Protestant Faith would be protected. Over one million left France. England benefited most and received generously, families of weavers, cloth makers, goldsmiths, silversmiths, shipbuilders and teachers. Many skilled in flax growing and the manufacture of linen went on to Ulster to the great benefit of that Province, and Calvinists swelled the congregations of similar worshipping Presbyterians.

Thrift and industry, respect for education and learning and a high dose of the Protestant work ethic made them an almost priceless gift to the future of the Ulster Plantation. At the Boyne, the defining battle of the Ulster settlers, there were three hundred Huguenot officers in King William's polyglot Protestant army; these refugees provided within two generations many lawyers, bankers, generals, admirals and scientists to the lasting benefit of what was to become the British Empire.

The succession of James II to the throne of England and Scotland was the beginning of the last act of the travails of Ulster before the wholesale departure to America. A very long last act; it began at James' succession in 1685 through to 1717, when the first significant number of ships set sail from Ulster ports to drop anchors in the ports on the Delaware River, mostly at Philadelphia, Chester or New Castle. James was an autocratic, unreconstructed, foolish Catholic who either knew little of, or did not understand, the English. His grandfather James I was called "The wisest fool in Christendom." That epithet was better earned by the grandson, although perhaps "wisest" was better replaced by "unwisest". To lose his throne in such a frivolous manner, and not even supported by the Pope. He set about imposing Catholicism again in Scotland, and most of Ireland, in a ruthless, clumsy way, and was forced to abdicate in 1688. Happily William of Orange, Stadtholder (King) of the Netherlands, had married Mary, daughter of James II. That suited the English very well and a Protestant monarch was secured when William accepted the English throne.

James left for France and came back in March 1689: landing at Kinsale near to Cork, at the head of a French/Irish army. Not for the first time was an invader to make the mistake of thinking that the route to defeating the English started in Ireland. The Catholic Irish were interested, but not interested enough. In the meantime, James' brother-in-law, the Irish Earl of Tyrconnel set about pacifying Ulster by dismissing all Protestant officers, magistrates and other non-Catholic officials. The Protestants rose up in revolt and barricaded themselves in the walled cities of Londonderry and Enniskillen. Both cities, defended by untrained men, remained undefeated by Tyrconnel's professional troops. The resistance of Londonderry has become the stuff of legend to this day, when the cry of "no surrender" will always bring out Ulster people onto the streets when they feel threatened by Catholics. It sounds *most* fearsome even when shouted today. In Londonderry the decision to deny entry to the King's soldiers – which was based on fear, misunderstanding, and the decisive action of thirteen hot-headed apprentices, who rushed round the city, locking the gates and lifting the bridge, while their elders and betters could not decide what to do – saved the city. Thus started the siege of Derry, as it was better known. Undefeated for 105 days, Tyrconnel withdrew. The Apprentice Boys Parade celebrates this famous act of defiance every year. This, the most famous of the annual Orange Marches, remains a flaunting source of Protestant ancestral pride, and for many Catholics an historical irritant.

With Ulster relatively secure, William's army landed at Carrickfergus with 10,000 seasoned troops and met James' army on the River Boyne on 1ˢᵗ July 1690. The Gregorian calendar later adjusted the date to 12ᵗʰ July, which is the day celebrated by the Ulster Orangemen. The army of William, now 35,000, made up of English, Ulster, Danes, Dutch, Germans, Swiss, Italians and Norwegians, all Protestants. James' army consisted of about 25,000 mostly émigré Irish, English loyal to James, French, German and some Swiss. The battle lasted most of the day but after the Protestants forced the river, James deserted his troops, fled to Dublin and then to France. Many noted with amusement that King William of Orange's Protestant success was greeted by the Pope and the Catholic Court of Austria with delight, as it infuriated Louis XIV, the supporter of James, but the political enemy of the Pope.

The Battle of the Boyne settled the fate of Ireland for the next 150 years, and that of Ulster until the present day. The 11,000 survivors of James' Irish Brigade went back to France and steady recruitment to it took place over the next 50 years. It is thought that during that time more than 450,000 Irishmen died in the service of France.

Many Scots, along with their ministers who had fled to Scotland at the approach of Tyrconnel's army, now returned to Ulster along with a fair number of younger men; and in the last 10 years of the 17th century there was a further 50,000 immigrants from Scotland. They were encouraged by the peace, the cheapness of farms and trade opportunities. Moreover they tended to be financially more substantial than earlier immigrants.

The Loyal Toast

Peace brought Protestants in Ireland of all denominations together in brotherhood, and there was a loyal toast widely popular in the first half of the 18th century. The accepted method of delivery was for the proposer to stand on his chair, put one foot on the table, and raise his glass to:

"The glorious, pious and immortal memory of the great and good King William not forgetting Oliver Cromwell, who assisted in redeeming us from Popery, slavery, arbitrary power, brass money and wooden shoes. May we never want for a Williamite to kick the arse of a Jacobite. And a fart for the Bishop of Cork."

This, followed by a reverential "Amen" from the company was the authorised shortened version.

Part two went "and he that won't drink this, whether he be priest, bishop, deacon, bellows blower, grave digger, or any other fraternity of the clergy; may a North wind blow him to the south, and a west wind to the east. May he have a dark night a lee shore, a rank storm and a leaky vessel to carry him over the River Styx. May the dog Cerberus make a meal of his rump, and Pluto a snuff box of his skull: and may the devil jump down his throat with a red hot harrow, and blow him with a clean carcass to Hell. Amen."

Bishop Browne of Cork, singled out so woundingly, was a great opponent of drinking and drunkenness.

8. Intermarriage

Four generations of Scots had settled in Ulster before the serious move to America began. It was another three generations before the tidal wave of emigration had subsided, though not ceased. In some 170 years of living side by side, it is inconceivable that marriage in some numbers did not take place. The evidence, if searched for, is there for the finding; and if not marriage, then cohabitation, for the hot blood of lusty youth will not be denied. On which side lay the greater prejudice? Plenty on both of course, but the greater probably on the Protestant, whose hatred of Catholicism was at a level equalled today only by Islam's detestation of the Jews. The Gaelic opposition was more economic than ecumenic. Not understanding, and perhaps not caring very much if the Protestants chose to worship the same God as themselves in a slightly different way; but caring very much to the extent of enduring hatred at the theft of their lands and loss of political liberty.

They were the same people, of the same blood and bone, even if it was necessary to go back two thousand years or more to consider the evidence. The differences were more nurture than nature. So who blinked first? Did the Scots start the intermingling or the Irish? Those most likely in favour were the Irish, even if resenting bitterly the contempt shown to them by the Protestants, mostly who believed that intermarriage would be sinful and cause loss of face. The Presbyterians, on the other hand, to whom bigotry had become an art form; and thought that a sexual relationship with a Catholic was an immoral act of such enormity that the perpetrators would end up in the Fires of Hell, would have opposed intermarriage. Marriages *did* take place. A young woman, or young man, displaying immense moral courage would then, as now, defy their families and marry. Even today, to marry except in your religion or caste is frequently a matter of great moment outside of the liberal Western world. Even in Ulster today, made worse by the 1920 Partition of Ireland into the Irish Free State and the Six Counties, and the vicious insurrection from 1969 to 1998, in which thousands of civilians, British soldiers and Ulster policemen were murdered, towns frequently divided into Catholic and Protestant sectors or, as it is more often called now, Nationalists and Loyalists. It is uncanny how a Protestant can recognise a Taig (a very obscene term) almost at a glance from his own people; and the accents are quite different, as different as New England is from the state of Georgia. Intermarriage also remains a painful business, which is almost unbelievable. Even worse, it is possible to encounter people from both sides of this divide who will admit to not ever having met socially anybody outside of their own religion. Not now out of hatred perhaps but indifference. The schools are as segregated as much as were the Southern States. So still, in 2005, a mixed marriage in Ulster may force the couple to leave Ulster, either for another part of the United Kingdom or for Eire, where prejudice has diminished.

The best evidence, factual as well as anecdotal is, that after Cromwell's New Model Army had turned much of the South into a wasteland, before discipline order and efficient administration was established, hundred of soldiers, Puritan Roundheads, settled permanently in Ireland, including Ulster, and married Irish Catholic girls. In no time at all the children of this misalliance were *not* Anglo Irish, but Irish. It has been said that the Puritan military conquest was rather less than the conquest of the soldiers by the indomitable spirit of the Irish women. It is a pity that no records seem to have survived of these marriages, but that they took place is accepted as yet another quirk of Irish history. A lovely side of the Irish nature is the skill with which conquerors were absorbed, then turned into patriots more Irish than the Irish.

When James I divided up the vast acreage of Ulster to create the Plantation, the Gaelic Irish were there in plenty and probably outnumbered the Lowland Scots by a factor of six or seven to one. Such Irish gentry as had remained, having survived the various wars and rebellions, were granted new leases, though usually of poor land, and many thousands of the landless peasants were employed on the farms of the settlers, both Scottish and English. There was thus daily contact of the closest kind between Protestant and Catholic. Not, it should be said, the contact of black slave with white master in the American South; nor the contact of black Kaffirs of Cape Colony in South Africa with the white Afrikaners. This was a mutually useful association of employer and employee, both members of the same ethnic group; the Gaelic Scots, who, when back in Scotland were only slightly less poor than the Gaelic Irish. The settlers needed wives, the Irish girls needed food, shelter and escape from grinding poverty. Religious barriers, though as formidable as medieval fortresses, were just as breachable. *Some* intermarrying must have taken place.

No legal barrier prevented intermarriage. Until the year of the Plantation, an existing law had forbidden intermarriage of Protestant and Catholic in Ireland. This was evidence of English efforts to segregate and subdue the Irish. The law was lifted in 1610, which they said was "To the great joy of all parties." If such was said, it is surely evidence that a mutual wish to marry existed, and with official blessing. The most persuasive evidence is to be found in the prevalence of Ulster names among the Scotch Irish in America. One finds O'Neills, O'Dohertys, O'Donnells, O'Hagans and many others. Some immigrants removed the prefix "O" and replaced it with "Mac" to improve the name's Scottishness. Sometimes the prefix was removed to give the name an English form, eg. Neill or Neal, and so obscure even further the ancestral origin.

The pastors and the priests played a central role; and in Ulster perhaps rather more than in the Southern Provinces of Munster, Leinster and Connaught. There were fewer Jesuits to influence the Catholic girls who wished to marry, and who for many reasons would accept the religion of their Presbyterian husbands. With this the pastors would have been content. The women, more down to earth, more realistic then the men, would have appreciated that the Scots were in Ulster to stay and the return of the land to the Irish unlikely.

So much for the "Pros"; but the "Cons" were very strong. If there is a single word to describe Continental Europe in the period 1550 to 1700, it is surely "cataclysmic". The religious wars reached heights of torture, executions, killings by sword, gun and arson not exceeded until World War I. King Philip II of Spain, by the time of his abdication in 1555, had burned, beheaded, strangled or buried alive 100,000 Dutch and Flemish Netherlanders; and why? Because they were Protestants. The Thirty Years War of 1618-1648 devastated Europe from the Baltic Sea in the North to Austria in the South. And what was it about? In simplistic terms, it was about Martin Luther falling out with Rome; the Reformation and thus the Counter Reformation. The English Channel, not for the first time, protected the English from the European conflicts but nevertheless there was religious conflict in Scotland and Ireland. That war was not between Catholic and Protestant but Henry VIII's Anglican Protestant Church trying to bend John Knox's

Presbyterian Protestant Church to its will. The four Stuart Kings fought hard but failed, Anglicanism failed. There were Martyrs, especially in that part of the Lowlands nearest to Ulster. So when the Presbyterian ministers with their congregation crossed the water, their faith had emerged intact from the crucible of religious persecution and was the stronger for it. They were ready to defend their beliefs in Ulster as they had in Scotland, against the heretical Catholics. Intermarriage with the enemy would be breaking faith with Knox, Calvin and Martin Luther.

From a different perspective the Irish Catholics viewed intermarriage with similar abhorrence as the Protestants. The Reformation may have cut a swathe through Europe and England but not in Ireland. The Jesuits, who had come at the bidding of Rome, had taken the Irish in hand and turned lukewarm Catholics into devoted servants of the Pope. As the Jesuits were fond of saying "Give us a child of seven; that is all we need." Irish patriotism was linked to Catholicism; for the English were not only political enemies but Protestant oppressors, who had tried to rob them of both political liberty and their Catholic faith. Be loyal to the Church, the Jesuits taught, and you will achieve political and religious freedom. So the Church became the religious *and* secular leader, and an Irish martyr became a Catholic martyr. Martyrdom, then and now, always inspired great loyalty in Ulster.

So religion rather than economic materialism provided the most resistance to intermarriage between the two people. When that is added to the physical danger of being surrounded, outnumbered by a resentful dispossessed enemy, the settlers may well sometimes have feared for their lives as they slept at night in their cosy homes. The slaughter of 1641 proved their fears to be right. Irish people were enemies to be watched, not neighbours to marry.

There is a parallel between the problem of Ulster intermarriage and that which confronted Americans in their contact with the Indian people. Race, with its taboos and language differences were barriers, but race does not always stand in the way of miscegenation. It did not in the case of Negro-white's relationships in the South. There were singularly few cases of white Americans consorting sexually with Indian women, who were kept securely at home by their men. Indians hated the whites and the women hated them also. Add to this the white hatred of the Indian, which was all the stronger for having robbed him of his country, his land and his way of life.

The later, if not the earlier settlers, would have brought their families with them. After a few years of the Plantation having been established, it would have been considered safe to bring the family into settled communities. In any case Scotland being so near, many men would have chosen to return home to find a wife. This sounds easier than might have been the case, and in the end, a man might have had to settle for *any* woman willing to make the trip to a troubled land. If the man was of an easygoing nature he might have decided on an easygoing unwashed Irish Colleen who might suit him better than a hard-faced Scottish scold, already on the shelf. Somebody made the point that the presence of plenty of English women in America was the chief reason not to mingle with the Indian, for which the Indians were no doubt grateful. Whereas the absence of Spanish and Portuguese women in the colonies to the South was the primary cause of racial intermix. The minister frequently travelled with a settler group, and he would be quick to set up a church, or at least a meetinghouse, where he could lay out the code of conduct, the do's and don'ts and prepare his Sabbath tirade against immorality, drunkenness and the dangers of slipping off the straight and narrow. The lecture on marriage and chastity would have been high on the agenda.

Lecky, the mid 19th century historian, Irish born and proud of his people, gave the consensus of scholarly opinion when he wrote "Most of the great evils of Irish politics during the past two centuries have arisen from the fact that its different classes and creeds have never been really blended into one nation, that the repulsion of race or of religion has been stronger than the attraction of a common nationality and that the full energies and intellect of the country have in consequence seldom or never been enlisted in a common cause."

If we accept the reasoning of Lecky, and he took many years writing on Irish history, the weight of evidence against intermarriage is strong. To the extent that it occurred, the Irish, that is the Catholic partners, seems invariably to have been absorbed by the Presbyterian Irish half.

King James had chosen well in persuading his countrymen to plant themselves in Ulster. A stronger bulwark against Popery and defenders of the Crown would not have been found in England.

9. Freedom of Worship and the Anglo-Irish Parliament

It could be said that with the victory of William of Orange at the Boyne, James II's permanent loss of the English/Scottish throne, and the removal of France for the foreseeable future as a military threat, peace settled over the whole of Ireland; and in particular Ulster. Whatever the problems the settlers might encounter in the next eighty-five years, the threat of war would not be among them. The problems of peace, whether political, religious or economical are what turned their heads westwards from time to time, to the Atlantic Ocean and beyond.

The threat of Papacy was laid low, and the decks were cleared for what came to be called the Protestant Ascendancy in Ireland. But this was not a Presbyterian, nor even a Puritan Ascendancy, but an Anglican, Episcopalian one, in the guise of the Church of Ireland. The membership of this Church, which was of course in communion with the Church of England, was made up of old 12th century Norman English, married into the Gaelic Irish, who had been Catholics for at least 500 years, and had then, in the time of Henry VIII mostly turned Protestant. Their numbers were then added to by English Farmers, tradesmen and landowners, who had bought or leased land from the Crown which had been confiscated either from the Irish or those Anglo Norman Irish who refused to accept the Anglican Faith, and surrendered their lands rather than lose the right of worshipping God as Catholics. The Protestant Ascendancy was to develop into a formidable power to rule Ireland for the next 250 years. To all the dissenters, Puritans, Presbyterians and others, the Ascendancy became the irritating stone in the shoe, the sand in the oyster.

Thousands of Protestants of all denominations who had quit Ireland for the safety of Scotland or England in the years before the Battle of the Boyne, returned after James II was vanquished. A Parliament was summonsed in Dublin, consisting of a House of Commons of 300 members, with 28 in the House of Lords; a replica of the English Parliament. The Lords was made up of 16 peers and 12 bishops. No room was allowed for conflicting constitutional or religious altercations. All members took an Oath of Allegiance to the King; made a declaration repudiating the Catholic Mass, transubstantiation and other Papist doctrines, and swore a second oath abjuring the spiritual supremacy of the Pope. The Catholic majority of the people had no voice in Parliament, and its armed Irishmen in exile offered no threat.

The Dublin Parliament was not absolutely free from London interferences, but operated on a very loose rein, establishing its own strong power base, while passing its own legislation. It had two main aims. Firstly to consolidate and expand Protestant land ownership. Secondly to so emasculate the Catholic majority which, though currently quiescent, would never have the resources to start an armed rebellion, or active insurgency. The first objective was met by creating a Court of Claims; the second by the progressive introduction over the next 40 years of Penal Laws; part punitive, part restrictive; so designed to lessen the Catholic capacity for rebellion. The Court was outraged by a promise made by the King to Patrick Sarsfield, the Irish Commander of James' invading army at the Boyne, to restore the rights of 65 of the larger Catholic landowners, which reduced the seized acreage by a quarter. The Court had brought actions against 4000 landowners declaring forfeit 1,100,000 Irish acres, an Irish acre being equal to one and a half English acres.

At the beginning of the 18th century, Catholic ownership had been reduced to one eighth of the total land available. In the next four decades it was further reduced. Conversion of proprietors to Protestantism, of the Anglican sort, some no doubt from religious conviction, but many through a tactical evasion of the Penal Laws, allowed many Catholics to retain their wealth if not their self-respect. Those Acts passed by the Dublin Parliament must have given dissenters, especially Presbyterians pause for thought. For although they were not aimed at them, the message was clear, Dublin could do whatever it wanted, and to whom it wanted. With no Parliamentary representation dissenters from the Established Church, though devout Protestants had nobody in authority to speak for them. As Jonathan Swift, that acerbic and witty Dean of St Patrick's Cathedral put it, remembering the great heroism shown by the Scottish settlers at Londonderry, Enniskillen and the Boyne: "The reward for loyalty to England is the privilege of being governed by laws to which we do not consent." How history does repeat itself; many New Englanders must have remembered Swift's words when in 1775 the cry went up "No taxation without representation."

With the peace, people felt safe, and the Presbyterian Church in Ulster began to establish its authority over the Scottish settlers. By 1690 there were nine Presbyteries and 120 congregations totalling 150,000 migrants and their descendants; at least three generations. At this time, many aspirants to office in the Church returned to Scottish universities to receive training as ministers. They brought back with them the "Westminster Confession," which defined the Presbyterian confession of faith, and was a viable alternative to the Thirty Nine Articles of the Anglican Church to which all the clergy had to subscribe. The Westminster Confession was regarded as "The most perfect written expression of the Christian Faith."

This codification of faith was a unifying cloak, which both enveloped the settlers and their families and gave power (willingly granted by the settlers) to the Church and its ministers. Members were devout and would travel as far as 40 miles and in great numbers to a Sunday service, so strong was a minister's influence, and so tight the discipline exerted on the willing worshippers. There was to be no shilly-shallying, no laxity as in the easygoing Anglican congregations. Such energy, such unquestioning belief and bigotry startled the Church of Ireland bishops to a religious danger or worse. By 1728 there were already 140 ministers to 600 Church of Ireland clergymen. However, as usual, matters were rarely as simple as they were expected to be. Ministers among the early settlers and their descendents in the early 18th century saw things differently to those who were university trained. They had adapted to the conditions imposed by famine, and grievous wars, and were known as "Old Siders". They did not take easily to the Westminster Confession with its acceptance of the Trinity. Nor did they consider themselves to be bound by it. "The Westminster Confession" they said "was man-made – not Christ-made; nor was it in the bible". Moreover, to them, all power came from God, and if he did not grant it, it did not exist. In the future it was university-trained ministers known as the "New Siders" who shook up the Old Siders.

This was subversive talk by the Old Siders, its secular discourse challenging the prerogative of the State. Invoking such concepts as the consent of the government, and the inviability of individual rights. No Government of the 18th century was going to stomach talk of this kind. The axe which fell on the neck of Charles I did not absolutely destroy belief in the divine right of kings; remnants of it remained. The Old Siders looked over the sea to England where dissenters had much greater freedom of expression, they thought, than in Ireland. The irony of this point of view would not have escaped many. To make matters worse, they attacked the conventional wisdom of the age that the interests of Church and state were the same. Religious domination determined access to political power, and that belief was as old as King David of Israel and Constantine the Great of the Romans. Hence the uprising of the Scottish Covenanters under the Stuart Kings which resulted in a Scottish Presbyterian Church without bishops, who traditionally were thought as puppets of the Monarch. Hence the American and French decisions to disestablish the Churches.

"Put not your faith in Princes or Prelates" was a useful piece of wisdom that spanned the centuries. King William and Mary showed love and tolerance towards the dissenters of Ulster, but their reign was short. William was killed in 1702 when his horse stumbled on a molehill. Their successor Queen Anne was totally in thrall to her Tory Governments, who were staunch Anglicans and considered it unpatriotic to be anything else. So in 1703 the Test Act was passed. This Act was called "persecution"; and so of course it might have been to those accustomed to 20th century religious freedom; but for the 18th it was nothing unusual. Most European statesmen of the time agreed that the interests of the State were best served by *all* the people worshipping in the same way, which should be the way of the Established Church, whatever that may be. In Queen Elizabeth's day all citizens were *commanded* to attend Church on Sundays and Holy Days, when the Book of Common Prayer was read. Religious wars in the 17th century in Europe were usually resolved on the workable principle that the people of a state was required to take on the Monarch's religion. Scotland at her Reformation established a State Church. The non-conforming Parliament in England during the 1640's had tried to impose Puritanism on the nation. The same strong spirit of uniformity prevailed in Puritan New England. So the Ulster Presbyterians were acting illogically and intolerantly in opposing the Test Act. For they, if *they* had had the power, would have denied non-Presbyterians the rights to worship differently.

However, those who refused to accept the authority of the Test Act were subjected to the severity of the law. In England it was less strictly applied and there were twelve dissenters in the House of Commons, and among magistrates, only a handful of whom were deprived of their rank. In Ireland and especially in Ulster, wherein dwelt most of the dissenters the Act was severe, and the Irish Parliament kept it on the statute book for 70 years. Right up in fact to the end of the huge exit to America Presbyterians and Puritans were expelled from all civil and military offices under the Crown, unless they were prepared to take the Sacrament of the Church of Ireland. Their political authority was reduced and another deep line of disqualification entered Irish life. The pity of it was that the Test Act was aimed at the Catholics of both countries; but the Church of Ireland saw it differently. To them, despite sharing a hatred of Popery, the Dissenters were a political threat, which can be translated into both a power and commercial threat. The Catholics were poor, cowed, lacking leadership, but the Presbyterians were none of these.

Ministers almost everywhere were turned out from their pulpits, threatened with the law. Since they now had no official standing, marriages they performed were illegal, and the issue of such illegal marriages, bastards. In parts of Ulster people could not bury their dead unless a clergyman officiated at the funeral and read the Established Church's burial service. Children could not be taught by Presbyterian teachers, for all dissenters were forbidden to teach. Moreover they had to pay the religious tithe to the Established Church.

"We have already seen how fatally the division between Protestants and Catholics has been aggravated by its coincidence with the division of classes, and how by a singular infelicity the same train of causes that greatly diminished among the lower classes the capacity for self-government made the higher class peculiarly unfit to be the guardians and representatives of their interests.

The Test Act was another great step on the path of division, and did much to make Protestant co-operation impossible."

That was the view of W E H Lecky writing in the 1870's and it summed up coherently and succinctly the unending troubles and tragedies of Ireland; and in the early 18th century the demon of Papistry was to some extent replaced by the intolerance and arrogance of the Anglo Irish Ascendancy.

10. Industry and Landlords

Years of intermittent war since 1641 had reeked havoc in agriculture and industry; but the peace which stretched from 1690 to 1798 was the longest period without war in Ireland's history. Perfect, one might think for the settlers of the Plantation to develop into an urbanised, industrialised, responsible people, and this was largely true. Growing cereals, especially oats and barley; raising sheep for meat, and wool for cloth manufacture; growing flax for spinning and weaving into linen, made for a full and active life in which the whole family took part. Irritants of course were ever present either of nature, politics or religion; but that was the stuff of life and could be dealt with.

An argument continued into the 1690's based on the Irish Cattle Bill of 1666. An innocent sounding name, but whose pernicious and spiteful effect was harming beef production over the whole of the island, as it protected English cattle farmers from competition. Mutton and dairy products were also included in the Bill. Even the burgeoning Irish linen industry was eyed warily by the English, who manufactured linen in a small way. It seemed to Ulster people that England possessed both the power and the will to crush any form of Irish industry when it suited them. Of course Ulster was not singled out. England did to Ireland no more than she had done to America and Scotland; acting in accordance with sound commercial principles that governed all colonial policy. It was a fundamental maxim that the commercial interests of a dependency should be subordinate to those of the mother country. Even the twenty-first century is not completely free of such practice. Jonathan Swift commented scathingly on the English when he said "They frame laws for the administration of kingdoms with the spirit of shopkeepers."

It was the rapid development of two industries, both new, to Ulster, woollen and linen manufacture which had grown swiftly in the last years of the 17th century; and which so alarmed the rival industries in England. Ulster had, in a few years achieved a remarkable prosperity. England could never make up its mind about Ireland's status. It was not like Scotland, which since 1707 had had equal status as a sovereign kingdom with England, sharing the same monarch. Neither was it a colony in the sense that New England was a colony. Ulster was an English Plantation, created as a bulwark against the Catholics of Ireland, and Continental Catholic attacks; yet it was treated as if it was a commercial enemy. Great efforts had been made to emasculate the woollen industry, and the Woollens Act of 1699 prohibited the exportation of Irish wool and woollen cloth to anywhere except England and Wales. Thus allowing England to establish the price without fear of competition. In modern parlance they rigged the market.

This setback was serious but not disastrous, because the second industry linen was about to receive a boost from the newly arrived Huguenots in Ulster with their modern methods of production and a propensity for hard work and sound commercial practice. Even before the Edict of Nantes, some Huguenots had read the runes correctly, or perhaps the writings on the wall, and quietly left France. Some joined the Huguenot officers in King William's army, and in Dublin where there was already a Protestant trade monopoly. Most were Calvinists who shared the legal restraints imposed on all other dissenters; but because they had no political ambitions, and their own churches, attracted no hostility from officialdom. At Lisnagarvie, a derelict village in County Antrim, a man named Louis Crommelin brought over 75 French weavers and their families, along with 1000 looms. From these grew an industry that became a major component in the Ulster economy.

The Huguenots were a unique people. Although seemingly self-contained and self-reliant this did not inhibit them from involvement in Ulster life; and were as well equipped a body of immigrants as a host country could wish for. They were an unusual mixture of experienced entrepreneurs and minor nobility, with skills difficult to find in Ireland, and plenty of capital brought out of France in the form of jewellery, gold and other portable valuables. Additionally they benefited from a strange provision in French Law that allowed exiles to sell property and take the proceeds of the sale with them. To safeguard family integrity, wealth was passed on from father to eldest son by primogeniture. Also the Irish Huguenots, as did those left behind in Europe, practiced "endogamy", by which the younger sons were required to remain celibate. Thus, except by bequests they had no claim on the family wealth. When the possibility of return to France was remote, the Huguenots abandoned endogamy, and integrated with the Irish, and other Protestants. From that point their contribution to the country's well being was formidable; especially in business, law, the military, science, architecture and ship building.

They founded the Irish banking system, and the Irish linen industry; moving it away from the cottage industry as it had been for several generations. The first bank was for themselves, started by David La Touche (La Touche is still a famous name in British banking and money circles) and it soon attracted others. The La Touche Bank was run privately for generations but eventually became the Bank of Ireland. If ever the expression "Protestant work ethic" could be applied to a single group of people *who* better than the Huguenots? Their contribution to Ulster's quality of life was founded on financial, commercial and industrial discipline backed up by probity.

After the Battle of the Boyne, the peace was not the uneasy peace of earlier decades, but the peace out of which grew faith in the future. The problems though were enormous and trade was terrible. Land and food were cheap, but there was little ready cash. It was linen that changed the way of life out of all recognition, and the growing of flax, the spinning, the weaving and the sale of the cloth created an integrated industry in which all the profits could be reinvested in the industry. Swiftly, from tenant farmers to landlords everybody prospered – even the Irish day labourers, though mostly landless – at this time, which preceded the English industrial revolution. The Irish linen industry was greatly admired throughout Europe. Exports grew dramatically, as the warring countries of Europe, their own industries affected adversely by conflict, bought huge quantities of Irish linen.

In 1700 England bought 12,000 yards
In 1704 700,000 yards
In 1710 1,500,000 yards
In 1728 450,000 yards
In 1740 6,400,000 yards

From growing the tiny blue flax flower emerged a society unknown in Catholic Europe, of producers, middlemen, retailers and services, including shipbuilding and port facilities to handle primarily the linen trade. Londonderry and Belfast grew to rival Bristol and Liverpool in size; and Belfast had a population of 8000 engaged in producing equipment for the linen trade, which had freed the Ulster settlers from the poverty and wretchedness which was still the lot of the rest of Ireland. With a certain rueful truth it was observed that "When the Scots came in 1609 Ulster was poor, and when they left, Ulster was rich."

There was, as is usual in a developing country, many ups and downs, with strong elements of feast and famine. In 1730 exports to England dropped to 3,800,000 yards. As British revenue commissioners restricted Irish linen because of a glut on the market; and to make matters worse, the price per yard decreased just as households were producing more on a falling market.

There was of course the American market. In 1705 Irish Tories had lobbied their allies in England to allow exportation to America. The Linen Act of 1705 did not harm *British* industry, but by allowing Ulster to export to America it discouraged the American linen industry. Export developed slowly but by 1741 the volume had reached 400,000 yards a year. At the same time Londonderry grew into the most important trading town in Ulster, largely through the importation of flax seed from New England and Pennsylvania. A elegant solution followed. Ships carrying cloth Westwards returned loaded with flax seed and bulky flax. This was handy to replace flax lost in the not infrequent bad harvests of Ulster. Also linen being less bulky than flax there was room on the outward voyage for passengers who had decided to shake the dust of Ulster off their feet and emigrate.

Bad weather? Yes, there was plenty. In succession 1726, 1727 and 1728 gave the most appalling harvests. All crops failed, pushing up the price of food so high that in 1729, also not a good year for linen sales, an Ulster minister witnessed "Such a dearth and scarcity of victuals as was never heard of in these parts. Almost the whole product of the last harvest is already spent and there is not enough seed to sow the ground."

The bad harvests in accordance with the rules of supply and demand pushed up food prices; but there were few buyers; cash was in short supply. This made it difficult for farmers to pay rent; but the landlord was in a cleft stick; it would be pointless to evict a tenant since nobody could afford to take over the farm anyway. Better an occupied farm and no rent than an unoccupied farm and *still* no rent. The evidence was now building up into a significant element when considering the merits of emigration.

It was during this period of bad crops and high food price all *over* Ireland – much worse in Connacht and Munster, that Jonathan Swift in 1729 penned his most savage satire against Irish Poverty.

A Modest Proposal for Preventing the Children of Ireland being a Burden to their Parents or Country.

I have been assured by a very knowing American of my acquaintance in London, that a young healthy child, well nursed, is at a year old a most delicious and wholesome food, whether stewed, roasted, baked or boiled. And I have no doubt it will equally serve in a fricassee or a ragout.

There was worse to come. In 1740/41, famine raged in Ireland (though not very much in wealthy Dublin), and it is said that 400,000 perished. Beyond doubt many thousands died, but 400,000? Such hyperbole is common in cases of massive catastrophes and good historians take a somewhat more cautious view of such claims.

In the far west and south of the Province, Ulster landlords had even less incentive to press tenants over rents. A Merchant from Londonderry explained in the late 1720s "Lands are everywhere fallen by 20 to 30 percent. I have myself some farmlands but 5 miles from this city, which was worth £45 per annum, and now the tenants' say it must be reduced to £24. So you may judge how it is likely to be with lands more remote from any large town." Western regions of Tyrone, Donegal and Fermanagh were sparsely populated. So pressing for rents would have ended with deserted farms. It sometimes happened that tenants left their farms as a ploy and the landlord offered a lower rent if they would return. The landlords were desperate to avoid buildings unoccupied and land returning to weeds and scrub.

Such a tenant/landlord relationship was rare with negotiating strength favouring the tenant. A similar situation existed in Medieval England after the Black Death, when the population had fallen by 25%. A shortage of labour gave the peasants a huge advantage when demanding higher wages. As a result the Parliament passed the Statute of Labourers Bill, which placed a ceiling on agricultural wages.

Bad harvests, good harvests, near famine, food glut, food shortages, high linen prices, ruinously low prices; and land prices all over the place may sound like hazards difficult to live with. But there was no war and crime was low. A very rough profit and loss of the period 1690 to 1740 would probably have shown that the tenant farmers, their families and Protestants generally had achieved standards of living way above those of previous generations. Moreover despite the various irritations inflicted by London and Dublin they felt themselves to be free men, a free people. Especially in comparison with the people of France, Spain and the various German states. Indeed, everywhere save England.

This gave the settlers confidence when dealing with the authority of every sort including the Presbyterian Church. Arguments leading to fights about seating places in church were not unusual, as seats tended to denote rank in the community. The rantings of the minister against alcohol and licentious behaviour were not always listened to with respect. Money in the pocket has always led to a lowering of moral standards. Sexual promiscuity was not unknown, and on public holidays and Fair Days, there was even talk of the "French Pox". Jack now reckoned he was as good as his master and as is not unusual, started to consider his position. Whether or not a step up the ladder of material success was not only possible but his right and his due. There was sometimes a few pounds tucked away for a rainy day; and the un-expired portion of his lease must be worth a few more – should he decide to move on; America for example. The English were about to get a shock. A shock that would not achieve its full effect before 1776, the start of the Revolutionary War.

11. The Ascendancy: The Anglo-Irish

The American people today may have a problem with the name "Scotch Irish". The British have the same problem with the name "Anglo Irish", perhaps more so. Just as the Scottish Irish, or Ulstermen – who flocked to America in their tens of thousands between 1717 and 1775, and then quickly took a leading role in public life: filling high ranks in the Revolutionary War against the British, in the Northern Army against the Confederate South in the Civil War of 1861-65, not to mention in the Confederate Army against the North in the same war – so the Anglo Irish provided field marshals by the handful, generals by the score and junior officers by the hundreds in the British Armies from 1690 the Battle of the Boyne, through Wellington in the Napoleonic Wars until the Second World War 1939-46. They bestrode Ireland like a colossus for 250 years. The difference between the two is that whereas the Scotch Irish deliberately tried (and succeeded) to conceal their identity within the melting pot of the American peoples, the Anglo Irish, the Ascendancy were consigned by history into oblivion.

Who were those people? The label suggests anyone of mixed Irish and English blood who lived in Ireland. Or were they by a narrower interpretation a particular caste, the product of historical circumstances who during the 18th, 19th and early 20th centuries were dominant in Irish affairs; distinguished by their culture, politics and religion? And if the alternative is correct, how was it that a fair proportion of this dominant caste were ethnically of Norman, Gaelic Irish, French Huguenot and Dutch origin; while some of the "native Irish" were of almost undiluted English stock? If the explanation of the ethnic mix is correct, and nobody seems to doubt it, it would not have been possible for the Anglo Irish *not* to have impinged on the lives of the Scots settlers, the body politic, religious and commercial core of Ulster; the Ulster Plantation. Thus to know the background of the Scotch Irish in America, a knowledge of the Ascendancy, as we will now call them (except when we are calling them the Anglo Irish) is surely mandatory.

In the years of their Ascendancy, the Anglo Irish were a small but elite body, a minority Protestant group spread throughout an overwhelmingly Catholic Ireland; a country of small material value but huge strategic importance to the security of England's Western flank. Denying invasion by sea to European Catholic Kingdoms hostile to Protestant England. The Ascendancy achieves a virtually complete control over the whole of Ireland, politically, religiously and commercially, becoming very rich on the way. It would be hard to describe this social elite in a few words for it was exasperatingly diverse; but a few that could be expanded into a very heavy volume would include arrogant, high minded, insensitive, devotion to duty, stupid, cruel, brave, elegant, artistic, clear thinking, kindly, politically pigheaded and eccentric beyond rational belief. They governed Ireland sometimes badly, sometimes well, and probably better in many respects than the present generation of Irish politicians give them credit for. If there was a common bond at all between the Irish Irish and the Anglo Irish it was the same affinity for horseracing, fox hunting, gambling and drinking. In the first year of the 21st century, the English have made hunting the fox a crime; but not so the Irish.

They left behind them a rich legacy of Georgian architecture; including in Dublin The Royal Irish Academy, the Royal Dublin Society, the Library of Trinity College. Cities abounded in which cultural and educational establishments are examples of the Ascendancy's respect for the arts and learning; an infrastructure of roads and railways attested their interests in modernity. They created also the political structure of a parliamentary democracy and a professional civil service based on the London model widely approved of by the Republican Government, which inherited it in 1921 and maintain it today. And course they left the English language; the Gaelic purists still try to maintain the Gaelic tongue as a second language, but not more than 5% of the people speak it.

Ireland is tiny. Its area is only 32,065 square miles; barely more than South Carolina's 31,195, it would fit comfortably in Indiana's 35,925. Yet out of this speck of land, cut off from the mainstream of European culture, the contribution of the Ascendancy from all the Four Provinces of Ireland; Ulster, Munster, Leinster and Connacht to posterity is astonishing. To literature they gave Oscar Wilde, Jonathan Swift, Burke Sheridan, George Moore, Goldsmith, W B Yeats, George Bernard Shaw, Samuel Becket and James Joyce. To soldiering they gave Wellington, Roberts, the Gough brothers, Wolseley and Kitchener. Many generals of the Victorian Wars, World War I and the bulk of British leadership in World War II,

Allanbrooke, Dill, Gort, Alexander Montgomery, Ironside, Templer and Dempsey. In both Irish and British regiments there were many soldiers who received the Victoria Cross, for outstanding heroism. The Victoria Cross is awarded rarely and usually posthumously; which suits British Governments as they thus avoid paying the meagre pension that accompanies the medal. A trawl through other waters retrieves other remarkable Anglo Irish: Bram Stoker who wrote Dracula, the Harmsworth brothers who changed the face of British newspapers out of recognition. Castlereagh and Edmund Burke in English politics. The higher ranks of the Indian Civil Service and other colonies of the British Empire drew heavily on the Ascendancy for its administrators.

Perhaps most bizarre was how the Ascendancy, most loyal of England's citizens provided Protestant rebels to free Catholic Ireland from English rule. They provided many of the leaders in the political and armed rebellions of the late 18th and late 19th centuries. Such men as Robert Emmett, Thomas Davis, Lord Edward Fitzgerald, Charles Stewart Parnell, John Mitchel, Padriec Pearce, and most astounding of all Wolfe Tone, founder of Sinn Fein (ourselves alone), which today is the political wing of the terrorist IRA and a powerful voice in Irish politics. Many of these men paid with their lives on the scaffold.

On the lighter side, and which surely owed much to the blood mix, they provided in disproportionate numbers, a spectacular array of gamblers, duellists, lechers, bigamists, drunks, spendthrifts and lunatics. What other social group on the whole of God's earth gave birth to such outrageous and outstanding examples of Adam's seed?

Fighting Fitzgerald

Fitzgerald was the supreme example of an Anglo Irish psychopath. The possessor of great inherited wealth, he was able to exploit privilege and exercise local power badly. Born in 1748, and related through his father to the Earl of Desmond and through his mother to the Earl of Bristol, who was also Bishop of Derry, Fitzgerald fought his first duel at 16. He married a sister of Thomas Connolly of Castletown House and on an extended honeymoon in England and France ran up debts of £120,000, fighting several duels on the way. He abandoned his wife and returned penniless to his father's estate in County Mayo. He formed the Turlough Volunteers, which he used as a private army of terrorists. Devoted to their leader, the Volunteers were prepared to kill anybody who annoyed him, but was not of sufficient social standing for him to deal with personally. His father was as spendthrift as his son, who did not like to see his inheritance wasted on drinking and gambling. To correct this tendency Fitzgerald chained his Father to a pet bear and later gaoled him in a cave. This escapade got him two years in prison and a £500 fine. A second conviction got him another sentence, but the Bishop, his uncle, got him off that and arranged for him to be made a Freeman of the City of Derry. In his inauguration speech he said that an ancestor had been a signatory to Magna Carta.

Nemesis finally caught up with him. He wanted to be colonel of the Mayo Volunteers; at the time commanded by Jack McDonnell, a Catholic lawyer. The Turlough Volunteers, now reconstituted and wishing to help him, obligingly murdered McDonnell. Fitzgerald was so patently involved in the murder that an exasperated authority tried him, found him guilty and hanged him publicly outside Castlebar Jail in June 1786. He was prosecuted by John Fitzgibbon, the Attorney General and later the Earl of Clare. Fitzgibbon and Fitzgerald had met before. They had fought a duel.

Ireland, unlike most of Europe, never became subject of the Romans, who took with them to all the subject countries Roman Law, Latin and Latin civilization plus those habits of national organisation in which they were pre-eminent. It was unfortunate that whereas the Norman Conquest of England was completed more or less in the single battle of Hastings in 1066, the fatal calamity in Ireland was protracted over 800 years. Anglo Norman incomers spread throughout the island, building their castles and towns such as Dublin, Limerick, Kildare and Wexford, and ending up more Irish than the Irish. The atrocities were regular, consistent and terrible and owed something to the old Brehon Gaelic Law in which the punishment for murder was a fine. The reign of Henry VIII was absolute, over all of the Four Provinces, but complete ascendancy dates only from the end of the punitive wars of Elizabeth, which broke the backs of the semi-independent Anglo Norman Irish chieftains, crushed the native population into the dust and established the complete authority of English Law.

The war conducted by Carew (see Munster Plantations in Chapter 6), by Gilbert, by Pelham and by Mountjoy was one of extermination. Today it would be called genocide. Prisoners, women and children, the sick and the wounded were slaughtered. The sword was not always found to be sufficiently expeditious, so the more painful death of systematic starvation was employed by burning crops and destroying stored food. Long before the war was terminated Elizabeth was told she had little to reign over save ashes and carcasses.

Ulster did not escape; Lord Mountjoy was merciless. The rebel chieftains McMahon and McArtmoyle offered to submit but were told neither could be pardoned without delivering the head of the other. The cruelties were by no means on the one side. A large number of soldiers in the service of England were Irish Catholics. English Rule brought with it two new and lasting consequences, the proscription of Irish Catholicism, and the confiscation of Irish soil; not so much confiscation as downright theft; but it was the 16th century after all. It should also be noted that the Irish chieftains, unlike their followers, were also largely indifferent to religious distinctions and the English cared more for the suppression of the Irish as a race than as a religious entity.

The Elizabethan Irish wars were not wars about nationality. The Irish clans had *never* fused into a single nation, nor had they wanted to. The devotion of the Gaelic clansman was to his chieftain. The Earl of Desmond, who was of the purest Norman blood, was supported by his Gaelic followers with the same fervour as was O'Neill, the Earl of Tyrone, also Anglo Norman, by his. The question of racial difference was never an issue. What stirred the Irish, noble or peasant, was the land and the conviction that they were being driven off their own soil, theirs for a thousand years. Even the Norman chieftains could not rob the peasants of their holdings; for by the ancient land customs of tanistry, as established by the Brehon Law, the humblest clansman was co-holder of the land with the clan chieftain.

In 1585 Sir John Perrot, a wise and tolerant English statesman, persuaded Connacht chieftains to surrender their lands to the Government, who would then lease them back in perpetuity by patents of the Crown in return for reasonable rents guaranteed by law, and the discharge of certain military duties. This gave them hereditary possession of both land and titles beyond dispute. Perrot succeeded with this plan only in Connacht, but it was a start. In the Provinces the English were determined to take the land by force, or by law weighted in their favour.

There was an uneasy peace until the night of 22nd October 1641, when a terrible war started. The Catholics, in despair, rose and started to massacre Protestant settlers in Ulster, and then in all four Provinces. Peace to the war torn land did not return until Cromwell, came over in August 1649, and confident he was God's emissary established a brutal but long lived Pax Britannicus. The job done, he left Ireland never to return. Punishments inflicted on the losers were severe, but there were no mass executions of either heretics or traitors to the Crown. A few Irish aristocrats were condemned and many lost such of their estates as were still left to them. Many though decided to submit to the Elizabethan Act of Uniformity, renounce Catholicism and accept the authority of the Anglican Church. This saved their lives, their family's lives, and their properties, and in due course they became stalwarts of the Protestant Anglo Irish Ascendancy. England was now in complete control.

Colonel Blood

Blood's eccentricities made those of Fighting Fitzgerald's seem almost normal. Dissatisfied with his land allocation after Cromwell departed, and blaming the Dublin Government, he decided to do something about it.

His first thoughts were to kidnap the Lord Lieutenant in Dublin Castle and organise a Protestant uprising; this, in a country controlled absolutely by Protestants. The Lord Lieutenant, the 10th Earl of Ormonde and the most grand of the Norman Irish nobility; the only Protestant in the grandest of Catholic Families, discovered the plot and Blood swiftly escaped to Ulster. There by posing firstly as a Presbyterian and then as a Catholic, he was treated hospitably by both, before moving over the water to Scotland. He lent a hand in some outbreaks of insurgency (on which side is unclear) before moving South to England. In Yorkshire for a time he earned a living freeing prisoners from the condemned cells. Later he professed to being a Quaker and was comfortably maintained by the Society of Friends. Once again his thoughts turned to Ormonde, now the Duke of Ormonde, who had come to his London House. This time Blood decided to kill him in the most dramatic manner; hang him on the Tyburn gallows, which were a permanent installation and in regular use. Ormonde returning from dinner in St James' was bundled out of his carriage; tied back-to-back with one of Blood's followers on a horse and facing backwards. Intending to gallop to Tyburn, close by, Blood rode ahead to put the rope in position. When the lynching party had not arrived, he rode back to check. He came across a struggle; Ormonde had thrown his rider, and the pair of them, still roped together, were conducting a curious trial of strength to a largely incurious crowd of passers-by. Blood cut his losses, tried to shoot Ormonde, missed, and decided it was time to leave. He now turned his fertile, if crazy, mind to the Crown Jewels, kept in the Tower of London. Partly successful, he made off with the Crown and the Orb, but dropped them in the street and was captured, then put on trial. He was so persuasive in his defence, that he not only received a Royal pardon from Charles II, but his estate in Country Mayo was restored to him, the loss of which had started the whole business.

Blood was ahead of his time, his raffish, ruthless amorality was more typical of the Anglo Irish bucks of the late 18th century than of his more puritanical time but a start had to be made sometime; he was a pioneer of a sort.

The 18th century was, for the Catholics, a period in which they were almost legally invisible. Bereft of elementary rights, punished for their religion, and with no say in how their country was governed. For the Ascendancy it was the most constructive period of their governance. 1691 to 1798 was the longest period that Ireland has known without war. It was identified by growing prosperity especially in Ulster; hampered occasionally by English constraints on trade, but sufficient to produce surpluses that kept the upper levels of society in comfort. Such wealth encouraged them to improve their surroundings, in houses, furnishings, gardens and such, the evidence of a growing, stable bourgeois society. It provided work for tradesmen and skilled artisans so that society benefited at several levels.

The Anglo Irish as a caste placed its stamp indelibly on the character of the Irish people, and on the physical nature of the towns and country, constructing for the first time public buildings of elegance, even of beauty, while the nation's nobility and squirarchy were putting up their handsome Georgian houses amidst broad acres of parklands, the first private and substantial houses ever built in Ireland (in the small County of Carlow there were thirty one), an orderly expansion of Dublin was in progress. Founded and colonised by the Norsemen in the 8th century, who turned it into a military and administrative headquarters, the Protestant Ascendancy of the 18th century gave it a dramatic architectural elegance; a superb heritage to which they are entitled to much gratitude. A traveller in England could wander in a dozen cities, and hardly remember one from another. He would have had no difficulty in remembering Dublin. It was the work primarily of four architects: two Anglo Irishmen of Norman origin, Burgh and Pearce, Englishman James Gandon of Huguenot stock (how often the name Huguenot appears in Ireland's history), and a German, Richard Cassels. Working independently they designed such notables as both Houses of Parliament, now the Bank of Ireland, a reconstructed Trinity College, whose most famous alumni included Jonathan Swift, savage satirist whose most famous book was Gulliver's Travels, Oliver Goldsmith, Edmund Burke, the politician, statesman and British Parliamentarian who staunchly supported America in the Revolutionary War; and of course Wolfe Tone.

Nobody doubts that culture was in short supply until the Anglo Irish wealthy, settled, comfortable in their skins, established and encouraged all the arts in 18th century Dublin. Burgh's gift to posterity is Trinity College Library, which houses the 9th century manuscript the Book of Kells. Cassels built Leinster House for the Earl of Kildare, and which later became the home of the Royal Dublin Society the National Library and the National Museum. Gandon built the Customs House, still one of the best sights in Dublin, and the Four Courts, badly damaged in the Civil War of 1922; shelled by artillery on the instructions of de Valera, the first President of the Irish Free State.

For something like 150 years this 3 square miles of Dublin housed the cream of the aristocratic, professional, commercial, legal and official classes of Anglo Irish Dublin society. Colonial administrators, rulers of millions in India, Africa and the Far East, retired to their Dublin homes amidst the familiar surroundings of their youth. The Ascendancy, some say, made Dublin the most beautiful, and intellectually the most stimulating city of Europe.

In time, attitude towards the Catholics changed, became more benign, particularly in the case of those who were still landowners and whose sons had been denied admittance to Trinity College and the professions. It was also in the minds of both Governments, London as well as Dublin, that unless substantial concessions were made to the Catholics, an invasion from France would trigger a rebellion to fight with the French. Foremost among punitive Acts aimed at Catholics were those to do with land ownership. The Bogland Act of 1771 allowed them to take up leases of 61 years on 50 acres of poor land provided it was at least one mile from the nearest town. Later, provided the Oath of Loyalty was taken, it was proposed to allow them to buy land with the same freedom as Protestants. This was *too* much for the Irish Parliament, but London insisted, and Catholics were allowed to move onto land with a 999-year lease. This concession was regarded as the first sod cut in the grave of the Ascendancy.

Other concessions were the right to bear arms; priests no longer had to be registered, but they were still denied the right to vote or to hold public office. The 19th century found the Ascendancy holding on to power by Parliament, by influence and finally by their fingertips as the move towards Home Rule, after the bloody rebellion of 1798 finally (though it took another 124 years) put the Irish Catholics in command of their own destiny. The Anglo Irish, as a caste holding political influence in Ireland finally came to an end in 1920 when the British Government handed power to the Irish Free State (still part of the British Empire) in 1920. In the six counties of Ulster however – the Protestant enclave, separate from the Irish Free State – the Ascendancy rule continued with the automatic election of Prime Ministers from patrician families until 1971 when Captain Chichester-Clarke became the last.

As for the Anglo Irish, many survive; some in their great houses – like the Guinness family, still immensely wealthy, with houses in Ireland, England, France and other countries owing to the world wide sale of Guinness, the best known beer in the world, others in their crumbling mansions, full of dogs and horses and symbols of several centuries of grandeur. England became the home of many, but most prefer the easygoing life in Ireland. They are to be seen on race courses, the Dublin Horse Show, the fox hunting fields, the fly fishing rivers. This strange wayward caste of eccentrics, more Irish than the Irish. Like old soldiers, (which many of them are of course), they never die, they simply fade away.

Lord Baltimore

A name not unknown in America; for his great, great grandfather, Cecil Lord Baltimore, founded the State of Maryland. The 18th century descendant however had interests somewhat different to his revered ancestor. A great traveller, particularly in the Middle and Near East, he was fascinated by the Ottoman Turkish Empire, though not by any means the theology of Islam. Of this he knew little and cared less. No, it was the Turkish socio religious practice in the matter of women. In short, polygamy, which to him made good sense; and he admired the way the Turkish upper class obtained them, kept them properly regulated and under control.

He adapted the Turkish system to the different circumstances of London, where he had a large house financed by the rents from his large Irish estates. On returning home he retained two London procuresses to find eight suitable young ladies; but for the regulation of his harem (for that is what it was), he followed the Turkish practice of importing two Nubian eunuchs, which seemed the sensible thing to do. Enjoying foreign travel and liking company, he moved around European capitals complete with his eight ladies protected by two black Nubian eunuchs. Celibacy did not agree with him. As one would expect, his arrival at some Grand Hotel in Paris, Rome or the like caused a few eyebrows to rise. In Vienna, an official, a cheeky fellow, asked his Lordship which of the young ladies was Lady Baltimore, and received the cold reply "A gentleman does not discuss his marriage with strangers".

12. Migration from Ulster - The Reasons Why

There was an increasing groundswell of discontent amongst the settlers. After 107 years from leaving Scotland, it did not seem that they were either completely accepted as trustworthy citizens by the Dublin Parliament or treated as well as they deserved by the Government in London. Moreover, the unrelenting hostility from the native Irish was hard to bear. Reasons for leaving, an action by comparison with which the departure from their Scottish village was as nothing must have been discussed far into the night in the presbyteries, the churches and wherever the settlers met. One would have had to search history for centuries to find a mass migration to compare with that of Ulster people. To find equivalent population movements, you must look to the forcible expulsion of Muslims and Jews from Spain in the late 15th century, when Spain and Christendom re-conquered the territory occupied by the Moors for 700 years. In Russia under Stalin, millions of Ukrainian peasant farmers were starved to death or moved a thousand miles from their homeland. Ulster differed by being a free movement of a free people: but it must have endured deep trauma. They could have stayed in Ulster, and, despite the vicissitudes since 1610, prospered from time to time; they would have done so again had they remained. The Ulsterman suffered none of the scrambled departures of desperately poor peoples who had experienced just about every kind of persecution to which a name could be put, sometimes with the sound of gunfire not far behind them.

What reasons drove them to migrate? Sound, cogent, more arguments in favour of than against? People do not just pick up sticks, and move on, unless goaded by something or other. Was it religious persecution of an irritating, rather than a cruel sort? There was no throat-cutting pogroms as meted out to 18th and 19th century Jews in Russia and Poland; or to the Armenians by the Turks in the early 20th century. Many survivors of those frightening times also ended up in America. There was a modest degree of intolerance shown by the Anglican Church towards Dissenters of all sects, but it would have been stretching a point to call it persecution.

Let us examine the question of religion. When the Scots made the short sea crossing, they brought with them hope of a better life, a promise of fertile land on long leases, and they brought their

Presbyterian way of worship. A benign King James of England and Scotland had invited them and promised to protect them. Presbyterianism against bitter odds, spearheaded by the Covenanters, had become the State religion of Scotland in due course, with its ministers trained at Scottish universities. Some ministers came over early in the Plantation, and gradually increased in numbers until the spiritual needs of their parishioners had been reasonably met. By 1620 the settlers had reached 50,000 plus a fair number of English; and by 1640 the numbers had reached 100,000. This was a very fast increase. Houses were built, villages developed along with places of worship. It grew as a civilized community, with the minister providing a stern control, to keep his congregation happy at worship and content at work.

It continued a united people, relatively free from English interference, until after the Battle of the Boyne and the death of King William. The Test Act was then passed by Queen Anne's Government in London. This was a critical, indeed traumatic event in the future fortunes of the Ulster Presbyterians. Their way of worship of their God came under attack: not so much in a punitive manner as administrative. Quickly the following actions followed.

All office holders in Ireland were required to take the Sacrament according to the prescriptions of the Established Church of England, the Anglican Church. This necessity, this order, fell heavily upon the leaders both spiritual and laymen of the Presbyterian Church, many of whom held posts as magistrates and other civic positions in Ulster. The irony was that the Test Act was aimed primarily at the Irish Catholics; but because of its rigidity, caught Presbyterians, and all other dissenters in the net. It was a "One size fits all" Act that was not only thoughtless but stupid. In England its aim was primarily at the Catholics; and the Puritans and other dissenters were afforded a measure of freedom. That is to say, a blind eye was turned on them, and there was little trouble. In Ireland it was different and the Church of Ireland which was in communion with the English Church, persuaded the Irish Government in Dublin to apply the Act in the letter but not in the spirit of the law, and it therefore fell almost as harshly on the Ulster settlers as on the Catholics. It was 1782 before the Test Act was repealed; by which time the damage had been done and there had been a collective will by the Ulstermen to vote with their feet.

Ministers everywhere were denied their pulpits and threatened with legal action. Ministers in many respects were outside the law, and any marriages they performed were unlawful, and any issue of the marriage were bastards according to the law. People could not bury their dead unless an Anglican clergyman officiated at the funeral, reading the burial service of the Anglican Church. Children could no longer be taught by the dissenting teachers. Many people of impeccable reputation were prosecuted in the bishops' courts as fornicators for cohabiting with their own wives.

With the application of the Test Act the Presbyterians must have thought neither justice nor gratitude was shown by London nor Dublin. They had supported Charles I against Cromwell's Parliament in the English Civil War, protested against the beheading of the King; defended Ulster against the last efforts of the Irish in 1641 to regain their lands, made the Plantation a success and Ulster prosperous for the first time in its history. The Presbyterian Synod at first opposed the Act but then dropped all opposition as it would have lost the annual grant known as the Regium Donum bestowed by Charles II. The Synod hoped for leniency in the Act's administration, but hoped in vain. James Froude, historian and at one time a clergyman in the Church of England called the actions of the Ulstermen between 1685 and 1690 heroic, and remarked ironically that "this was an insufficient offset against the sin of nonconformity. When the native race made their last effort under James II to recover their lands, the Calvinists of Derry won immortal honour for themselves and flung over the wretched annals of their adopted country a solitary gleam of true glory. Even this passed for nothing. They were still dissenters, still unconscious that they owed obedience to the hybrid successors of St Patrick, the prelates of the Establishment; and no sooner was peace re-established, than spleen and bigotry were again at their old work."

The case for migration on religious grounds was strong enough, but there were other, more compelling reasons. Throughout history, religion is, more often than not, quoted as the cause of wars, but through the mists of belief, unbelief, heresy and dissent, the real reason for war is uncovered – land. That finally is the driving force, the *casus belli*; possession of another nation's land. There used to be a question put to the senior history class in English schools when history was regarded as important. It was "The Thirty Years War 1618-1648, was it the last of the religious wars or the First of the national wars? Discuss". At least from that date onwards there was never any doubt what war was about, and it was never religion; even if both sides claimed to have the blessing of God on their side.

Land, the freedom to own it, or to rent in perpetuity; and the freedom to trade on the basis of possessing the land. Attacks on both these freedoms were rarely more than a generation away from the Scottish settler from the time he arrived in Ulster to the time of his departure. Land allocation was generous, King James had kept his word. Leases were usually thirty-one years, much, much longer than in Scotland, but leases and the ability to pay even a reasonable rent were, from time to time, at the mercy of both weather and the market. Decent weather was needed to produce food and flax to make linen. When the weather was bad, cash became short but the landlord was still entitled to his rent. When times were good, harvests bountiful, and plenty of customers for grain and flax, the landlord wanted more rent, especially if the lease was about to expire, and there were those willing to pay the higher rent. This practice was known as rack-renting, and from the landlord's point of view and in fact present day practice economically sound. Because of the long leases, tenants mostly improved their holdings, improved buildings and land; and by the end of the second and third decades of the 18th century, many thirty-one year leases came up for renewal more or less at the same time. Rack-renting naturally took place all over the province. The tenant farmers, justly or unjustly, were outraged, and some felt they had little choice but to return to Scotland or go to America. This is a point of view hard to believe; the serious thinking about packing up to go elsewhere must have been accompanied by more pressing matters. Nevertheless, such stories were common currency. Then occurred one of those amusing quirks of fate. Some native Irish saw in the present situation a splendid chance to own, or at least rent some of their own land. Six or more would club together to buy the new lease made available by a settler deciding to quit. Archbishop King, an Anglo Irish churchman who loved Ireland, writing in 1719 just after the first wave of Scotch Irish emigrants had sailed to America, was sure that the land question was the real cause of the exodus. He wrote:

"Some would insinuate that this is in some measure due to the uneasiness dissenters have in the matter of religion, but this is plainly a mistake; for dissenters were never more easy as to that matter than they have been since the Revolution [of 1688-89] and are at present: and yet they never thought of leaving the kingdom, till oppressed by excessive [rents?] and other temporal hardships: nor do only dissenters leave us, but proportionately of all sorts, except Papists. The truth of the case is this: after the Revolution, most of the Kingdom was waste, and abundance of the people destroyed by the war: the landlords therefore were glad to get tenants at any rate, and set their lands at very easy rents; they invited abundance of people to come over here, especially from Scotland, and they have lived here very happily ever since; but now their leases are expired, and they obliged not only to give what was paid before the Revolution, but in most places double and in many places treble, so that it is impossible for people to live or subsist on their farms."

To make matters worse, rather than renew the lease of a tenant who *could* pay, the landlord would offer it at an even higher rent to cattle raisers who could earn more profit from meat than arable crops. The tenants were even more bitter when the landlord was permanently absent and the property was managed by an agent. Absent landlords were an insult made worse by rack-renting. Tenants were accustomed to dealing face to face with a landowner who had a moral obligation to deal with them fairly.

Then there was the interference in trade by the English Government, frequently acting through the Dublin Parliament in which the Plantation settlers were not represented. This was done through several Acts, which seemed to have been designed to protect English farmers and factories against Ulster competition in particular, and Ireland in general, for example, the Staple Act of 1663, which prohibited the direct exportation of anything except horses, provisions and indentured servants. In 1699 the Woollens Act prohibited the exportation of Irish wool and cloth to anywhere except England and Wales. This left all other markets to the English who could then virtually fix their own prices. This practice was harsh and damaging to Ulster. Hardly less damaging to the Province's trade was the Irish Cattle Bill of 1666, which prohibited the export of cattle, mutton and dairy products to the English market, to protect English farmers, who clearly had plenty of influence among the Members of Parliament. The majority of the Members would have been landowners, some on a vast scale, and they would have considered it their duty to protect *their* tenant farmers.

In the matter of linen, the English Customs watched Ulster warily in case their output and price structure damaged the small England linen industry. It was a constant irritation to Ulster when England flexed its powerful mercantile muscles in its own protection. Ulster was after all a province of England: not a colony. It was like the sheep farmers of the County of Kent in the South being protected by the Government against competition from the sheep farmers of the County of Yorkshire in the North. Add rack-renting and restrictions on trade to religious discrimination, the case for migration was surely made and preparations either individually or by groups started.

There were five significant waves, with some lesser movements in the intervening years, before 1717 and after 1775. The seminal movements were 1717-18, 1725-29, 1740-41, 1754-55 and 1771-75. It was a case of an irresistible force distinctly not met by an immoveable object. The Government seemed supine and uninterested in an event that many might call cataclysmic for England in view of what was to follow after 1776.

1717-18 The Trail-blazer

After four successive years of drought, serious preparations for departure began. Ships were chartered, discussion groups sprouted, and sales of property began. In 1717 more than 5000 made the voyage to the American Colonies. It was not an adventure into the unknown. Since the 102 Founders of the Plymouth plantation who voyaged in the Mayflower in 1620 without tools, seeds or in some cases their wits, ships regularly made the passage from England to New England. The ships had hardly changed in construction, discomfort certainly had not changed, nor had the hazards of the Atlantic Ocean. But at least most voyages had been completed in safety, with few deaths, and those who were about to make the journey would know about the fortunes of those who had preceded them by 100 years and be comforted by the news that would have travelled back from Delaware, Maryland, Pennsylvania, Virginia, New England and other places.

Encouraging reports had filtered back, from William Penn's colony, of cheap fertile land offered by well-established authorities on agreeable terms. Cheerful, optimistic information made the risks worth taking, despite the capricious weather and some danger from epidemics such as smallpox. What matter; if an uncomfortable, and most certainly crowded voyage of 10-12 weeks ended by meeting with welcoming hosts, the sacrifices which were not small would have been worthwhile. The initial drawback of how to finance the crossing troubled many, but was easily dealt with by the adventurous. When there was no other choice, indenture could easily be taken up; it was already a well established practice and large numbers agreed to it. It was hardly slavery (as they would quickly find out) to work for an American master for a fixed number of years under conditions laid down and protected by English Common Law. At the end of the apprenticeship, the man was free and well equipped with knowledge and tools to make his own way anywhere in the Colonies, a farmer or tradesman without let or hinder, a free man as he had never been before. Many chose that route; few regretted it.

That wise Anglo Irish prelate Archbishop King wrote to the Archbishop of Canterbury in a letter of 1718 summing up what lay behind the emigrations and asking him to use his influence on the English to make them accept the damage being done to the fabric of Ulster.

"I find likewise that your Parliament is destroying the little Trade that is left us. These and other discouragements are driving away the few Protestants that are amongst us. No Papists stir except young men that do go abroad to be trained to arms with intention to return with the Pretender (James II). The Papists being already five or six to one, and a breeding people, you can imagine in what conditions we are likely to be."

As to 1718 it is difficult to know how many made up the total of the first wave, but King said in that year thousands of families had gone. Reports from Philadelphia said that twelve or thirteen ships had arrived that summer. New England also reported the arrival of many ships, some with smallpox, between 1714 and 1720.

1725-29 The Tidal Wave

This was so large that even the English Government noticed it; and a commission was set-up to investigate the reason for the mass immigration. Such numbers threatened the loss or at least an unacceptable reduction in the size of the Protestant community. That of course is what Archbishop King tried to tell them in 1718 when he wrote to Canterbury. Rack-renting was given as the principal reason for the Tidal Wave, and that may well have been so; but there were other causes too. Indifferent harvests put up food prices; money was *very* short. Poverty was widespread throughout Ireland for Jonathan Swift to write "Whoever travels through this country would hardly think himself in a land where either law, religion or common humanity was professed, with the old and sick every day dying and rotting by cold and famine and filth and vermin." But whether Swift was writing about Ulster people or Catholic Irish is not clear. The latter is most likely, for reasons that except in extreme circumstances would never apply to Protestant people.

There was no evidence reported of the arrival of shiploads of emigrants in distressed conditions. Certainly not by James Logan, the Secretary of Pennsylvania Province and a Quaker from Ulster. He wrote in 1729 "Last week no less than six ships arrived, and every day two or three also." Letters from Hugh Boulter, Archbishop of Armagh in 1728, are also revealing as to the prevailing conditions. He wrote that food was scarce and dear, and was one good reason to quit. On March 13th of the same year, he wrote "There are now seven ships, each carrying about 1000 passengers, ready to leave Belfast." And on November 23rd he wrote "About 3100 left this summer, and the worst is, only Protestants are going which badly affects our linen industry in the North."

Miserable scenes were enacted of wholesale ejections, of the disruption of family ties, of the forced exile of men who were passionately attached to their country. Lord Carteret, Viceroy in Ireland, an enlightened statesman, vainly deplored "the great evil that England inflicted on its own interests in Ireland", and urged the Presbyterian ministers to use their influence to abate it., failing, it seems, to appreciate that it was the ministers that suffered most from the Test Act.

1740-41 The Force of Famine
You do not need to search much before finding the reason for the third Exodus; the appalling famine which struck the whole of Ireland in 1740. Ulster was affected as much as the other three Provinces;

and no goad could have been more painful, or inflicted greater damage. They say 400,000 died in these two years. Accurate? Perhaps; who did the counting? No matter; what is sure is, many, many thousands died in Ulster, and tens of thousands in the rest of Ireland.

How is it possible to imagine such catastrophe in all its horrific magnitude? In the whole of England's history there is no record of famine that extended to a tenth of the Irish Famine of 1740-41. Nor for that matter in the rest of Western Europe.

This third wave differed from the first two in that its immigrants on arrival mostly moved to the South West from Pennsylvania, which had shown great generosity to all those who sought refuge. They took the trail through the Great Valley into the rich Shenandoah Valley of Virginia, which led on to the Carolinas. In the years of 1728-1750 records suggest that Ulster lost one quarter of its trading cash, and a quarter of its population. If that was true, the quality and calibre of the people who departed, by their action inflicted great harm on the Province of Ulster; yet no blame could be attached to them. The provocation that drove them out was too heavy to be borne.

1754-55 Help from America

Droughts of the most calamitous variety hastened the gathering of goods and chattels and movement to the docks of Belfast, Londonderry and lesser ports of departure. It is a mystery how a province as rich in rain as Ulster should ever had had drought at all; but the weather of the time was well recorded. Droughts apart, there was also a thoroughly modern reason to hasten the escape – propaganda. A succession of Carolinian Governors, of which two were Ulstermen, appealed to the Province to send many more immigrants to whom a great welcome would be accorded as the Carolinas were short of manpower. This appeal did not fall on stony ground. Governor Dobbs of North Carolina reckoned that as many as ten thousand landed at Philadelphia in a single season, most of whom ended up in his state. Then for the duration of the French and Indian Wars, the rate of arrivals slowed. Strangely, this coincided with a period of economy recovery in Ulster, when the incentive to migrate lessened. This prosperity was so extensive that the gap in the settler population was filled by the arrival of people both from Scotland and the other Irish Provinces.

1771-75 The Marquis of Donegal lends a hand

As had happened before in Ulster, the economic recovery was followed by depression, and many of the newcomers from Scotland and the other provinces elected to leave for America. Another reason was equally powerful. In 1771 many of the long leases (31 years) on the Marquis of Donegal's Antrim estates came up for renewal more or less at the same time; and the rent increases were so huge that, either the tenants could not pay, or the anger was so intense they decided to give up and leave. During the next three years nearly one hundred ships sailed West carrying perhaps 25,000 Presbyterians and other dissenters – a figure that by many is considered to be very conservative. It had become difficult to find enough ships to deal with the flood of escaping settlers. It is also said, though on meagre evidence, that this huge departure was paid for by the settlers, and not by signing on as indentured labour. Many had been working in the linen industry, which had always paid good wages; and many were small farmers owning their own land which they were able to sell for cash.

The propaganda to encourage emigration came not only from America. When it *did* arrive, by word of mouth or by letters, or even American newspapers, it was taken up by interested parties such as ship owners, or their agents, and inflated to give, undoubtedly, a very optimistic view of what the future held in America for those brave souls prepared to make the voyage. It was every salesman's dream, a settler's market. Scouts for the ship owners did not wait for the passengers to appear, they sought them out the length and breadth of Ulster to tell the tale of the pot of gold awaiting them in the Shenandoah Valley. Many of the agents worked directly for prosperous Americans who wanted indentured servants to work on their land and in their houses.

Despite abuses – it would have been unusual had there been none – the system of indentured labour helped the strong but needy to make the move to the new country – the New World, as it was still sometimes called – and gave the colonies the much needed manpower. Free men entered freely into an agreement binding on both sides, a splendid system of which the developing nation would look back with pride. Pennsylvania the Quaker State perhaps benefited more than most as the nature of their already settled towns and established farming systems easily absorbed men to work the land and women to work in the house. The master would be honest, fair and ready to reward diligence and initiative. In 1700 the Legislature listed as rewards, at the termination of the period of indenture, two sets of clothing, a new axe, two hoes; and under William Penn's own regulations, the freed servant was entitled to 50 acres of land. It was not unknown for some immigrants to choose indenture even if they had sufficient means in order to learn the American way of life at small cost.

Other Colonies fell short of the good Quaker practice and fairness. In the South where black slaves provided most of the labour, indentured servants were treated in accordance with the letter rather than the spirit of the law. Paradoxically they were less regarded than a slave, as a slave was a commodity to be preserved, whereas the servant was free at the end of his indenture. It would not have been unusual for a few scores to be settled when the time came to end what might have been a less than pleasant relationship.

The indentured servant saw nothing humiliating in the system; there was no stigma of bondage, and freedom was guaranteed by an honestly administered law. When the ship reached the port of discharge, and this may well have been the immigrant's choice, there was a sale and Colonists made their bids. The period was usually 7 years, but sometimes only 4, and the rights of the servants were clearly established, especially those concerned with his entitlements at the expiry of service. It was not abnormal to apprentice oneself in the Colonies; but beginning in 1728, by far the greatest number came from Ireland. From 1717 to 1775, for 58 years, it is thought that at least half if not two thirds of Ulster immigrants entered America to become indentured servants. The rest would have been able to pay for the passage and support themselves by offering their labour or buying their own business in trade or farming.

By 1775 about 200,000 (as far as is known – some say 250,000, others 300,000) had entered America, . Throughout the Great Migration, religious liberty had always been a motive; but only in the early stages. It is nevertheless significant both for Ulster and America that the majority leaving Ulster were Presbyterians. Few Protestants who took communion with the Established Church of Ireland were migrants to America, and Irish Roman Catholics almost none; their time had not yet come, and *would* not until the 1850's. It is astonishing that the Catholics did not go in hordes, if only to escape their poverty and servitude. They seemed more tightly bound to Ireland and their ancestors. The English historian James Froude says that the migration robbed Ireland of the bravest defenders of English interests, and peopled the American seaboard with fresh flights of Puritans. He wrote:

"Twenty thousand left Ulster on the destruction of the woollen trade. Many more were driven away by the first passing of the Test Act. ... Men of spirit and energy refused to remain in a country where they were held unfit to receive the rights of citizens; and thenceforward, until the spell of tyranny was broken in 1782, annual shiploads of families poured themselves out from Belfast and Londonderry. ... Religious bigotry, commercial jealousy, and modern landlordism had combined to do their worst against the Ulster settlement. ... Vexed with suits in ecclesiastical courts, forbidden to educate their children in their own faith, treated as dangerous in a state which but for them would have had no existence, and associated with Papists in an Act of Parliament which deprived them of their civil rights, the most earnest of them at length abandoned the unthankful service. They saw at last that the liberties for which their fathers had fought were not to be theirs in Ireland. ... During the first half of the eighteenth century, Down, Antrim, Armagh, and Derry were emptied of their Protestant Families, who were of more value to Ireland than California goldmines."

Many of the late arrivals of the 1771-75 wave, were men of substance, but what mattered were not the goods a man came with, but his character and adaptability in crisis. As pioneers or adventurers the Scotch Irish could not have been bettered; they were prepared to go beyond the established towns to the frontier, and then on into unknown and dangerous territory.

13. The Celts Reach America

America may not have been the Promised Land of the Israelites, nor the Atlantic Ocean the Red Sea. Nor did they need to wander for 40 years in the Wilderness before they, the Ulstermen of Ireland, the Scotch Irish, became an important part out of all proportion to their numbers of what within 200 years was to become the greatest nation in the world's history. The Atlantic was more the River Jordan than the Red Sea, though 1641 to 1717 could be in a more modest way be considered the Wilderness Years, as they survived wars, famine, evictions, government interference, hard times, and attacks on their right to worship according to the teachings of Knox and Calvin. The welcome received where ever they landed was, on the whole, warm. Were they not after all encouraged to come to swell the manpower, since at least 1681 when William Penn received his charter from Charles II to create a sanctuary for Quakers?

As James Murray from County Tyrone declared in a letter to his minister back home. "This is a bonny country, and aw things grows here that ever did I see grow in Ereland. We has Cows and Sheep, and Horses plenty here, and Goats and Deers, and Racoons, and Moles, and Bevers, and Fish and Fowls of all sorts. A Lass gets 4 Shillings and 6 Pence a Week for spinning on the wee wheel."

The fruit of Jacob's loins was 70 souls according to Exodus Chap. 1:5 as he obeyed the cry "There is corn in Egypt" and went there. When, 430 years later, they fled the wrath of Pharaoh, no doubt the numbers had swollen to more than a few thousand. This was as nothing to the 250,000 or so Ulstermen who departed more in sorrow than in anger from the land that had nurtured them for better or for worse between 1710 until the final wave in 1775. The population of America in 1776 has been put at 2 1/4 millions, of which the Ulster element has been put at 10-25%. A huge margin for error of course, but if we accept 12% it still may be totalled 270,000.

How different from Ulster must have Pennsylvania seemed, to have caused one migrant to call it "A large land of Liberty and Plenty." As they sailed up Delaware Bay in fine warm weather; high mountains in the distant west; covered with tall cedars; Relief and optimism must have been their first thoughts, looking back on the bleak wintry landscape of Ulster. They had reached journey's end: the ports of Chester and New Castle where the Schuylkill

River flows into the Bay and Philadelphia. This was not frontier territory. This was as settled as Boston and other New England towns whose development was now 100 years old, and well known to the English. The Ulster mindset was clearly on the middle colonies, and only secondly on the Eastern seaboard; while the Southern colonies of Virginia and the Carolinas had not even been considered. Perhaps the Presbyterian obsession with liberty and freedom prejudiced them against slave owning colonies, even if later they were able to rationalise their attitude to slavery. Also of course the Church of England was strong in the South, a Church which to the Presbyterian was almost as ungodly as the Catholic. Maryland was worse; it had been founded in 1634 as a Proprietary colony by the second Lord Baltimore, who had become a Catholic and made Maryland a Catholic refuge. Many Scots Highlanders fled there after the disastrous 1745 rebellion.

No doubt some of the voyagers on the ships of 1717/18 were coming as indentured servants, and would have been content to stay in the ports of landing; but the farmers among them wanted small farms, not the huge tobacco plantations of Maryland. The New Englanders, though Calvinist and Puritan, gave a cooler reception and did not exactly kill the fatted calf. Nevertheless, many from Scotland or Ulster first made homes there before, in what was to become a hallmark, their restless fashion, moved South to Pennsylvania in search of cheaper and more expansive land. At the time they did not recognise this was the prelude to crossing the Western Frontier into unknown and dangerous territory. But for the moment they were to relish the fine climate, civilised society and land for purchase. Looking at earlier Irish history it is puzzling why Catholic Irish whose living conditions and political future were so appalling did not flock to the Catholic refuge of Maryland.

When going to America was discussed it was about taking ship to the port on Delaware Bay and then North into Pennsylvania. For the whole of the Great Migration of 58 years, the majority entered America through those ports of Philadelphia, Chester and New Castle. History records accurately that the orderly mass movements of 1717, 1732, 1740 and 1760 were to Pennsylvania, Virginia, North Carolina and South Carolina. Dispersion to other ports such as New England, New Jersey and New York was but a fragment of the whole. By the census of 1790 the dispersal percentages had altered somewhat, and the water was muddied by the difficulty of separating Ulster Scots and the Scots who had come from Scotland; two parts of the same tribe, but by no means the same people.

Penn, like many leading Quakers, was as shrewd as he was devout. He turned his attention to Germany to augment his domain with hard working, pious and disciplined people, and as early as 1683 a few families came from West Germany, though the majority of Germans came much later. Naturally they were mostly Lutherans, good sound Protestants. The character difference between the two classes of immigrants were quickly noted, and not always to the advantage of the Irish, who were regarded as irregular in working habits, reckless, quick tempered and inclined to drink, and by no means the best of farmers. The Germans on the other hand had a reputation for hard work, frugality, abstemiousness and apolitical except at the local level. That there were differences is undeniable and these ultimately contributed to the country's benefit. The fiery Ulstermen defenders of the frontier and pioneers of the West. The quiet Germans, deep thinking, homemakers and town builders. It takes all sorts to make a great people. The stubborn Irish character was recognised early by James Logan, Secretary of Pennsylvania when he invited the Ulstermen to come "As his own countrymen, defenders of Londonderry and Inniskillen," as likely defenders against the Indians. He was right, but there were moments when he must have wondered if he had not bitten off more than he could chew, especially when they started to show more interest in the spirit of the law than the letter, a keener interest in natural justice than lawyer's justice. Squatting on a nice piece of land saved both time and argument. In such matters Logan found relief when dealing with Germans.

Poverty is relative, but by the standards of Pennsylvania the immigrants, or most of them, were poor. Some had a little money, others not, and it was the latter who came out as indentured servants wanting to be placed in households. The others were land hungry farmers. Land *was* cheaper, if you had money. The few who had enough could buy 5,000 acres for only £100. Others could buy 50 acres for as little as one penny an acre. Land could hardly have been cheaper, but it still did not discourage squatting, which caused problems and massive irritation to the colony's administrators who wanted land sales to be both orderly and fair, and not decided by squatters' rights. Perhaps the officers of the state were excessively bureaucratic. With so much land available the farther you moved West towards the Susquehanna River, the squatters alleged "It was against the laws of God and nature that so much land should be idle, while so many Christians wanted to labour on." The shrewder officials however felt the farther the Irish moved West away from the nest-building Germans, the less likelihood of civil war breaking out. "it was no use Logan complaining" they said "The colony had begged them to come. They did, land was plentiful, and it was not unreasonable they should have it, money or not, provided they were prepared to clear the forests and farm on it." The logic might have been suspect, but a sitting tenant takes some shifting if he is one of many. Where many were neighbours they resisted vigorously any attempt to evict. Ugly incidents sometimes occurred with agents of the state, resulting in cuts and bruises on all sides.

Thomas Penn, son of William, arrived from London in 1732, perhaps disturbed by news received from Logan that all was not well with the Scots Irish, and concerned about his family's interests. The Penns were the Proprietors of Pennsylvania after all and perhaps Thomas had lost some of his father's concern with brotherly love and natural justice. Anyway, he started a campaign of evictions, and the collections of money owed. Logan *had* been lax but perhaps he was wiser than Penn, and knew better than him the combative nature of his fellow countrymen.

It is true that many Germans preferred the comfort and protection of established towns, but by no means all. At the same time as some Scotch Irish staked out their claims on the Frontier, a few Lutherans were never far away. Just far enough away to enjoy the comfort of their own language. The Irish went to one side of a river valley and Germans to the other. The next year another batch would arrive, passing through the established settlement, to repeat the process of being together – but separate. It was the same in western Maryland, in the earlier days in the Shenandoah Valley of Virginia, and afterwards into the Carolinas. Groups of each nationality, cheek by jowl, but not mixing; separated by the formidable barrier of language; and apparently with no commanding reason why any sort of relationship should be struck.

The Great Valley of Pennsylvania winds in a wide arc from the Delaware River to the south-west, with to the North the Appalachians rising from fertile soil and miles of rich farmland. The Susquehanna bisects the state neatly with many tributaries flowing from it. Each with its own valley giving the pioneers many choices in which to stake their claim, however illegal, for a cabin, a forest to clear and land to plough. To Philadelphia, Chester and Bucks, the original counties, Lancaster was added in 1729. These touched on the disputed territory of Maryland, and the border was not finally fixed by that famous duo of English surveyors Charles Mason and Jeremiah Dixon until 1763-67. Many years later the term Mason-Dixon Line would become notorious worldwide in the fight to rid America of slavery. Philadelphia was a market town on which the counties of Chester and the other three depended for supplies. Later Lancaster served the same purpose for those heading for Virginia. It became what today would be called a service industry centre; from blacksmith to food and drink: cattle markets to which cattle were driven from as far away as North Carolina.

Between 1720 and 1730 Scotch Irish had settled along the eastern bank, both North and South of John Harris. The Appalachian foothills, the goal of many a pioneer, could only be reached by crossing the river to go West. He had already built a trading post alongside his house, so he added a ferryboat service, big enough to transport families and their goods across the Susquehanna. Harris's Ferry became famous, and an indispensable link on the Great Philadelphia Wagon Road, which extended finally to upper South Carolina. With the passing of time Harris's Ferry became Harrisburg and John Harris an honoured name in American History.

North of Harris's Ferry in the upper portion of the Cumberland Valley, there were Scotch Irish whom story writers described as "People of the better sort". Rich and gracious, so they said. The writer Wayland Dunoway calls it "The most important single Scotch area in America." The seed plot and nursery of their race, the original reservoir which, after having filled to overflowing, sent forth a constant stream of immigrants to the northward, and especially to the South and West. For a generation other racial groups were but scantily represented.

John Harris

There is always somebody in a community who is outstandingly useful and prominent in the affairs of the people. Such a man was John Harris, a native of Yorkshire, who built himself a house beside the Susquehanna in 1705. Yorkshire men are not unlike Ulstermen: argumentative, combative and competitive: bad losers. They say you can always tell a Yorkshire man, because you can't tell him anything; one hundred percent perfect for the frontier.

As the Cumberland Valley became settled so did the State Proprietors (that is to say the Penn Family) became uneasy. Indian territory was dangerously close. In fact a few squatters were already over the border and likely to provoke an incident. The touchy settlers did not seem over-worried but were, according to the Proprietors, completely out of control. There is an analogy with the situation in Ulster during many periods of the Plantation: except that there the land taken from the native Irish was first confiscated (or if you prefer it, stolen) by the English Government for redistribution to the Scottish planters, as a matter of policy. The difference in Pennsylvania and other American Colonies was that Proprietors who had been granted land charters ownership by the English Crown tried to be scrupulously fair to the native Indians across the Susquehanna, by buying their land not stealing it. That was the theory; but inevitably there was a limit to the amount of land the Indian Chiefs could sell without betraying their own people. Ultimately pre-emptive occupation would be followed by compulsory purchase; take it or leave it. That is what in the end happened, and caused the terrible raids and wars with the Indian tribes from 1754 until well into the 19th century. The Scotch Irish merely anticipated a circumstance that everybody knew was going to happen as night follows day. They led, others followed.

The colony leaders in Philadelphia found themselves on the horns of a dilemma – in modern parlance, between a rock and a hard place. In good faith they had made promises to the Indians when white men were few on the ground. When the immigrants arrived from Ulster *and* other places too, hungry for land and, as they saw it, natural justice, and whose presence would enrich the state, what should they do? They did what politicians throughout history have always done; they sided with strength, and in the fullness of time there would be no shortage of lawyers to make them feel free of blame.

If the Ulster settlers were at fault it was at least partly due to an almost unnatural restlessness. Though many thousands remained where ever their first home had been made, many others packed everything except the log cabin and moved on; all too frequently into western territory that would put them in dispute with the colonial administration and thus with the Indians. Firstly across the Susquehanna into the Cumberland Valley; later South and south-west into complete virgin forest and plain.

Virginia and the Carolinas.

Pennsylvania, within 50 years of its foundation, was full of newly arrived settlers, from Germany, Ulster and even New England, who came to plough the land and build villages and towns. Virginia, 130 years after a few English reached the James River was empty; except for the Indian. True, there were some English; but they were wealthy planters of tobacco, their servants and their black slaves, occupying the coastal Tidewater lands. The vast acreage of the rest of Virginia, notably the Shenandoah Valley, was empty, except for the nomadic Indians. It was not until the first decades of the 18th century that the Governor and others considered inviting immigrants to settle in the back country. Thinking like wealthy landowners, which they were, they sought companies rather than small farmers, to develop huge estates. They, the companies, would be responsible for finding the settlers. In 1701 estates as large as 30,000 acres, free of taxes for 20 years were on offer provided that within two years there should be one well armed man for each 500 acres with a fort in the centre. Later 50 acres were offered free to any man to settle in the back country. Few of these generous offers were accepted, for the Shenandoah was too remote, too dangerous and too far away from supplies points.

It was the arrival of the Ulster settlers from 1717, peaking in 1730, that started the flow from the North across the Susquehanna at Harris's Ferry, and from Chester and Cecil counties in the Chesapeake Bay area into Maryland. German settlers came also but in small numbers. As a measure of numbers that came and settled permanently in the Shenandoah Valley, two counties Augusta and Rockwell claim to be the most Scotch Irish in present day USA. The seedbed of settlers was the Cumberland Valley of Pennsylvania, but the plants flowered in the Shenandoah. Strangely, in the early days more Germans settled in the northern end of the Valley; but two huge grants of land made by Governor Gooch in 1736 brought in a positive avalanche of Scotch Irish. The sheer size of these grants is mind-boggling. One of 118,000 acres went to William Beverley in the County of Orange between the great mountains, which contained the Shenandoah River. The second was made to Benjamin Borden, an agent of Lord Fairfax, and was for 500,000 acres along the headwaters of the Shenandoah and the James Rivers.

There is an interesting link with George Washington attached to this grant. His half-brother Lawrence was married to a lady of the Fairfax family; and in 1748 Lord Fairfax employed George to survey his vast property. These two land grants were so full of Ulstermen that by 1746 the region was known as the "Irish Tract". The power and the patronage attached to the ownership of such huge land-masses played a significant role in the development of Pennsylvania and the Southern colonies. King Charles II (1660-1686) made a grant of land to Lord Culpeper totalling 5 million acres, from whom it was passed on to the Fairfax family. Surveys later show the Fairfax land to cover over 8,.000 square miles in the Valley and to the west of it.

There was another man, James Patton, who served both Beverley and Borden in bringing settlers to their land. He was an Irishman of the seafaring sort, having served in the Royal Navy. He prospered, and owned a ship with which he traded between England and the Rappahannock River; claiming to have made twenty-five Atlantic crossings, carrying pelts and tobacco East and shiploads of Ulstermen and their families West. These mostly arrived in Pennsylvania but lost little time in making their way to Virginia.

The third great surge of the Immigration Wave was 1740-41, the years of famine, sickness, and a winter so horrific it was called "The time of the black frost" because the ice was black, and the sun rarely seen. This large migration went through Pennsylvania almost without pause directly to Virginia, where free land was more prolific than East of the Susquehanna. Squatting was the order of the day as the surveyor and lawyers were a long way away in their urban comfort. The seemingly never ending stream of Ulster migrants poured South as far as Roanoke where the Shenandoah Valley ended and they took the fairly easy route in a generally southerly direction to North Carolina, under the leadership of that man of many skills, James Patton, and established the counties of Pulaski, Wythe and Montgomery. Still in Virginia, but not far from North Carolina where the rumour was that hundreds and thousands of acres were there for the asking, and settlers warmly welcomed.

If there was a problem, perhaps a leading problem among many, it was the lack of spiritual guidance. The pioneers were too numerous and too deep into wild country to attract other than brave, adventurous and devout Presbyterian ministers. There were not enough of such pastors, and they were sorely needed. Since the first Scots quit Scotland in 1609 for Ulster, the Church was never far behind, and continued to strengthen the structure of worship, discipline and education which gave the Church such influence with the people, and cohesion in prayer and action. The people and the minister were accustomed to be in harmony and mutual respect. Praying like good Calvinists, living like good Christians, disciplining the family, listening to the minister, and working hard like a Protestant. Of all those desirable moral attitudes, only the last was not in short supply. They badly needed a minister's lashing tongue. Despite the evangelism of the Presbyterian minister Francis Makemie from 1683 along with a few others in the Eastern port of Virginia, the colony was pitifully short of ministers in the 1730's and it was after 1740 before the First Presbyterian Minister set up in the Shenandoah where the Augusta Stone Church, and the Tinkling Spring Church were opened. The Church of England was of course long established in the coastal and tobacco planters area but would have been regarded with contempt by the Ulster people. Under persuasion from the Synod of Philadelphia in 1738 complete religious toleration was guaranteed by Governor Gooch.

The third wave continued South, in the Carolinas, into easy open country, and although the majority was still Scotch Irish they were joined in South Carolina by Huguenots, Calvinist refugees, originally from France but probably just arrived from Ulster. The most interesting group were the Catholic Highland Scots. Seemingly immune from Calvinism and Protestantism, they fought for the Catholic Bonnie Prince Charlie, claimant to the English and Scottish Thrones. Having given the English a bad fright in 1715 they were badly beaten at Culloden in 1745. To escape English revenge, those who could went abroad, many ending up in the Catholic refuge of Maryland, and the Carolinas. Most of them spoke only Gaelic and had little intercourse with the Scotch Irish. But they prospered like most immigrants. In the Revolutionary Wars their loyalties split. Those who hated the Presbyterians who aided the English against them in Scotland supported the Crown: those who hated the English more than they hated the Presbyterians fought for the Rebels.

This influx of immigrants landed on the South Carolina coast, through the thriving port of Charleston, to settle mostly in the coastal areas. Few went up country. Few arrived by way of the Great Philadelphia Wagon Road, which stretched from Philadelphia to the Yadkin River in Virginia, some 435 miles, and finally to the Savannah River, a total length of 700 miles. The settling of the Carolina Piedmont owes much to three exceptional governors of North Carolina between 1734 and 1765. They were Gabriel Johnston, a Scot from Dumfries-shire, Mathew Rowan and Ulsterman and Arthur Dobbs, born in Carrickfergus in Ulster. The settlers arrived in their tens of thousands, mostly in the West in the lee of the mountains, coming from Pennsylvania by the popular route and became a tightly-knit collection of Presbyterian Calvinist communities, which in due course became a formidable source of recruits for Washington's Army.

Thousands more came out of Pennsylvania by way of Harris's Ferry and other crossings, into the Cumberland Valley then South to the Shenandoah and on into North Carolina, Scots Irish still in the majority, but with plenty of Germans. The Scotch Irish included not only raw immigrants fresh from Ulster, but second generation young men, chafing perhaps at parental authority and wanting land of their own, where it was both cheap and plentiful. Just as the shippers' agents in Ulster made attractive overtures to the Ulstermen, so the agents of Beverley, Borden and Lord Granville, still a mighty Proprietor in North Carolina encouraged the Pennsylvanians to come West and South.

It was surprising that the steady movement through Eastern Pennsylvania across the Susquehanna, to the Cumberland Valley; then South into the Shenandoah Valley of Virginia, and then south again into North Carolina had met no more than sporadic Indian resistance. That was to change in 1754 when serious trouble erupted. The Indians started to oppose with violence and mayhem further penetration into their ancestral hunting grounds. There were ten years of bloodshed. Many white men, women and children were killed, sometimes massacred, and no quarter was given on either side. Indian uprisings were so widespread in Pennsylvania as to halt immigration from Europe for the best part of ten years; and it was a further 100 years, more or less, before the Indian Wars stopped.

The Founding of Maryland

There was a man, George Calvert, a Yorkshire man, secretary to James I, who did some "planting" during the Ulster Plantation. He was created Lord Baltimore, became a Catholic in 1625 and retired from public life. James then asked him to seek out a colony in America as a refuge for his fellow Catholics. He looked at Newfoundland and decided it to be too cold, and then came south to Jamestown, but felt unable to sign the Protestant Oath of Supremacy there. Later Charles I gave him a Charter to settle in the Chesapeake area. It was his son Cecil, the second Lord Baltimore, however, who organised the settlement in 1633.

Cecil recruited seventeen sons of Catholic gentry to lead and finance the enterprise, taking with them as intermediaries 100 settlers, mostly Protestants, some of them married, a few farmers and two Jesuit priests. They went in two ships, the Ark and the Dove, both heavily armed, and there was great opposition from political and religious enemies to sabotage the expedition. Cecil's brother Leonard was appointed Governor, assisted by two Catholic gentlemen, Jerome Halwey and Thomas Cornwallis, whose task was to get on well with the Virginians, using the Protestant intermediaries. Religious toleration was accepted and practised. A town was to be built and they had to be able to feed themselves and train a militia. One of the priests, Father Andrew White, kept records which recorded the foundation as an exemplary success, and he wrote "This baye is the most delightful water I ever saw. Fertile, plenty of fish; woods of walnut oak and cedar. There are strawberries, rasberries, deer, ducks, eagles and herons. The place abounds with pleasure and profit."

The colony was called Maryland after Charles I's wife, Henrietta Maria, and the town St Mary's. They traded in axes, hoes and cloth for 30 miles Inland. According to English Law Baltimore colony was a feudal Fiefdom, answerable only to the King, but owning all the territory with political and judicial authority, belonging to Lord Baltimore and his heirs.

The principal investors got 2,000 acres each. Anyone bringing less than 5 men got 100 acres plus 100 acres per man other than himself. Married settlers got 200 acres plus 100 for each servant. Widows with children got equal grants, and the land was freehold. Those with no money could pay for their passage by accepting a 4-year indentureship, agreed and signed by the ship's captain, who then sold the agreement to bidders on landing. On completion of the 4-year term, the man received 50 acres and a year's provision of corn. Maryland was a text book example of how a colony should be run, and in quite a short time was wealthy with plenty of tobacco and grain for export.

Bitter hatred on both sides confirmed the white man's belief that "The only good Indian was a dead one."

The Quakers of Philadelphia struggled vainly to persuade the white settlers of the merits of negotiation rather than fighting: to turn the other cheek occasionally, rather than repay aggression with aggression. But that was not the way of Ulster Presbyterians who, in the matter of defence looked rather to the Old Testament Gideon, than the New Testament Sermon on the Mount. Worse, they were inclined to get their retaliation in first.

It was known as the French and Indian War; the French were clearly rousing the Indians to rebellion. The English saw it differently as no more than a side issue in the greater conflict with France of the Seven Years War, 1756-63, which was being waged in Europe, mainly in the German States, and out of which, ultimately, would emerge the victor in Canada, and thus America. The Redcoats sent out from England, along with the white American colonial soldiers, among whom was a certain George Washington, a distinguished officer, and finally Commander of the Virginian Militia, settled with the French at Quebec where they were routed by the British under the young General James Wolff, killed in the battle. From that point onwards France ceased to take further military action in America, except for minor help during the Revolutionary War, with the provision of huge amounts of military material to be used against the British, and the blockading of Yorktown with the French Navy, which forced the British to surrender to Washington. The French aid is considered by historians to have bankrupted France and hastened their own Revolution.

Raids didn't quite cease with the British capture of Fort Duquesne, cutting off the Indians in Ohio from the East. In 1763 Pontiac, the Indian chief in Ottawa province, brought many tribes together, to launch an attack as massive as it was unexpected on the Pennsylvania settlers, killing over 2,000 and causing mass panic. Thousands fled the frontier areas and in Virginia several settlements were slaughtered by the Shawnees, creating scenes of unforgiving revenge and horror.

Pontiac's war ended after two efficient expeditions into Ohio territory. If war teaches anything, the Pontiac business taught America the fighting qualities of the Ulster Scotch Irish immigrants and their willingness to take independent action in their own defence. Winston Churchill said of the British at the end of World War II "In war resolution; in defeat defiance; in victory magnanimity; in peace goodwill." If you cut out "magnanimity" and "goodwill" he could have been referring to the Scotch Irish in the Indian Wars.

The Scotch Irish seemed to have been singled out for obloquy, especially by those insulated from the frontier by distance and urban security. Germans especially kept well away from Indian fighting. Many others including Rhinelanders seemed to have the same distaste for war on religious grounds as the Quakers. This is somewhat surprising as post Eighteenth Century at least, showed the German speaking peoples to be extremely military. On the other hand the British, who included Ulstermen and Scotsmen, were always and still are a martial race, to whom the irregular nature of the frontier war suited them very well. There is a difference between "military" and "martial" that is not always understood, and the Indian Frontier turned out to be a suitable if bloody training school for fighting the Revolutionary War not many years hence.

The great victory over the French brought the American colonialists closer to their British cousins and British Crown than ever before. They had fought shoulder to shoulder against a common enemy. Loyal subjects of King George III, members of a vast Atlantic Empire, British rights and liberties united the Protestants who had come of their own free will from England, Wales, Scotland and Ulster as never before. Celebratory bonfires were lit in Boston, Charleston and Philadelphia, and the British Redcoat clapped on the back as a "Damned fine fellow."

That was as town citizens saw it; relieved the Redskin had been kept at bay on the frontier. But the Frontiersmen saw it differently. They declared themselves "Loyal Subjects of the best of Kings, our rightful Sovereign George the Third." Free men and English subjects, their status was regarded as no more than marginal in Pennsylvania. Little power and influence in an Empire in which they rightfully considered to have played a significant part in fashioning and defending, they resented not being better regarded. Perhaps they felt like their ancestors in Ulster, who fought so bravely before and at the Battle of the Boyne in 1690 and received little thanks for it. This had in due course contributed to the decision to go to America.

The Indian Way of War

"His method of making war is never manly and open. He skulks in ravines, behind rocks and trees; he creeps out in the night and sets fire to houses and barns. He shoots down from behind a fence the ploughman in his furrow. He scalps the women at the spring, and the children by the roadside, with their little hands full of berries." Anon.

The Frontiersmen had their own way of waging war, which had little in common with 18th century European wars; or so we are told. They fought fire with fire. If the Indians scalped, they scalped. If the Indians butchered they butchered. If white women and children were killed, they killed Indian women and children without mercy. If indeed the Old World did fight chivalrously in their wars, such luxuries were denied to the Frontiersmen who wrought desolation far into Indian territory; and who is to say they were wrong?

Writer and poet Rudyard Kipling, who admired the British soldier (Tommy, as the Germans called him) wrote the poem "Tommy Atkins", which could equally have been written about the Scotch Irish frontier fighter.

"For it's Tommy this and Tommy that, and chuck him out the brute.
But it's 'Saviour of his country when the guns begin to shoot.
An' it's Tommy this an' Tommy that an' anything you please;
An' Tommy ain't a bloomin' fool – you bet that Tommy sees."

Danger still lurked and the settler soldiers could not be other than prepared for the Indian raids. They were edgy, nervous, trigger-happy perhaps, and so acts of savagery *did* take place. As always the coin has two sides. On the front the Scotch Irish was fine and resolute, but on the reverse sometimes brutal. In December 1763 a group of rangers in Dauphin County heard a rumour that the peaceful Conestoga Indians in adjacent Lancaster County had given aid to hostile Indians. Acting on the rumour fifty of them rode to the Indian settlement in Conestoga Manor, and believing also that one named Bill Sawk had murdered a settler, found and murdered six Indians and burned their cabins. On hearing of the attack, the fourteen survivors were put in the workhouse under protective custody. Two weeks later, the Frontiersmen left a tavern on the Donegal Road, and battling through snow and ice entered the workhouse to finish the job. All fourteen were butchered with tomahawks and scalping knives. A local man saw two children aged about three whose heads had been split with tomahawks, and scalped. Several women also had been similarly treated. One man's legs and hands had been cut off and a rifle discharged into his mouth. Thus was the legend of the Paxton Boys born.

After the Conestoga massacre (and there is no other word to use), the Paxton Boys learned that the Quakers were gathering Indians together for their protection. Believing the state authorities cared more for Indians than for the settlers who had suffered death and mutilation at Indian hands for 10 years or more, this enraged them further. So an undisciplined mob of about 200, dressed in their eye catching skins and moccasins set off for Philadelphia, roughing up numerous law-abiding citizens on the way. Walking through Germanstown, swearing and shouting, rounds were fired through windows. It took the presence of Benjamin Franklin to calm them down with a promise to look into their grievances.

The actions of the Paxton Boys were considered outrageous and received scant sympathy. In fact their conduct was compared unfavourably with that of local Indians. They were dismissed as "the lower sort of people"' little better than servants working in Donegal and Paxtang (which was the township of the Paxton Boys). Another comment was "an ignorant and enthusiastick Mob of Presbyterian traitors." Benjamin Franklin was a severe critic and called them "The Christian White Savages of Peckstang and Donegall." Every community in troublesome times need scapegoats and the Paxton Boys were convenient and available, and had received no protection from the Government. There would be many more occasions over the next 150 years when the people, feeling a lack of natural justice, took the law into their own hands.

A Presbyterian minister, stung by the verbal attacks from what he considered to be a corrupt Government, issued a stern warning "Any settler would be obedient to Government when they give me Protection. When I am not protected nor can they expect me to be Obedient." Among the Scotch Irish as a whole there was a fair degree of satisfaction, as their fierce resistance on the frontier released more land, more quickly for occupation. But among the great and the good of Philadelphia and other towns, their radical actions verged on anarchy: a danger to good and civilised government. In short the Quaker and other Christian pacifists became fearful of the Scotch Irish. It took the Revolutionary War to restore them to the ranks of "Good Americans." The frontier fighting interfered with the Great Migration for a while, and it was 80 years before significant numbers of Germans started to pour in again. The Ulstermen though, hardly waited until conflict quietened before the ships from Londonderry and Belfast started to enter Delaware Bay again.

This ditty was addressed to the Philadelphia Quakers by the Paxton Boys.

Go on, good Christians, never spare
To give your Indians clothes to wear.
Send 'em good beef, and park and break.
Guns, powder, flints, and store of Lead,
To shoot your neighbors through the head.

It is sometimes forgotten that when the Seven Years War ended in 1763, the French ceded huge territories to the British West of the Alleghenies. This complicated the already difficult problem of allocating lands, as the farther the Frontiersmen moved West (some were already in what had been French territory *before* the end of the War) the less they were inclined to accept colonial authority. The British, anxious to support the Pennsylvanian Government, issued a Proclamation banning settlements in the new territories. The Appalachian Range was a natural boundary, and in general the body of settlers accepted that, and did not venture further West until the conclusion of the Revolutionary War on 19th October 1781 at Yorktown.

After that, there was no stopping them. Farther south there had been some penetration, through the Cumberland Gap in Southwest Virginia as soon as it was discovered. Kentucky and Tennessee probably had their first settlers in 1770. There was a deluge westwards from 1782, which was in some ways a seminal year. The Scotch Irish as they broke through West of the Cumberland Gap lost their virginity as it were, and became Americans. No longer Irish, Ulster or English, or even Pennsylvanian or Virginian, just American. It is doubtful if the name Scotch Irish was used among themselves by 1800 in Kentucky or Tennessee: or as far west as Mississippi by 1813. The banner of their Ulster origins if waved at all would have been in the Carolinas, Virginia, and points East and North of the Shenandoah. If waved today it is not done aggressively. There is no need. They are comfortable in their skins. They are American; no need of secondary identifying names like the Catholic Irish Americans or the Italian Americans, or the African Americans. It is unthinkable that those of English descent should call themselves Anglo Americans. The Scotch Irish, one feels take the same view. Of course back in Ireland in the province of Ulster, it is different; there they are Ulstermen, and why? Because they feel threatened by the Catholic Republicans, a minority in Ulster but supported by the Catholic Republic of Ireland; who, until a few years ago, refused to accept the existence of Ulster as a separate province of Ireland. In fact, the British Labour Government may wish the Irish Question would disappear, and Ulster might agree to be ruled from Dublin. What irony, the British wish to divest themselves of the most patriotic part of the United Kingdom! *That* will never happen; not while the blood of the Scotch Irish Frontiersmen runs in their veins.

The Lesser Settlements

Pennsylvania, Virginia and the Carolinas became the homes of the vast majority of Scotch Irish who arrived in the period of the Great Migration of 1717-1775. But far from insignificant numbers were to be found in the others of the original thirteen colonies, not to mention the Scots who arrived direct from Scotland. By no stretch of imagination the same people as those who came from Ulster, the two being separated by almost 200 years of being at one time the same people. Nurture had, as it sometimes does, triumphed over nature. As Oscar Wilde said of Britain and America "Two peoples separated by a common language." Emigration from Scotland during the Eighteenth Century reached a quarter or more of that from Ulster. After the Union of the Parliaments of England and Scotland in 1707, the two nations had equal rights, which included freedom to move anywhere in the British Empire. For the best of reasons, many chose to go to America. Some went as indentured servants, some to escape from harsh living conditions, others because of land enclosures, which robbed them of their land. Many Catholic Highlanders fled Scotland after the defeat by the English at Culloden in 1745; and many were exiled to the penal settlement in Georgia. Strangely, many of the Highlanders remained loyal to the Crown; even stranger, it was the Presbyterian fighters of the 1745 rebellion who remained loyal. The Scots mainly did not seek their futures beyond the frontiers; they tended to migrate to Eastern towns, where they turned themselves into phenomenally successful businessmen.

Five Ships arrived in Boston during August 1718; they were
The "William and Mary", James Wilson: Master, out of London.
The "Robert", James Ferguson: Master: out of Belfast.
The "William", Archibald Hunter: Master, out of Coleraine.
The "Maccallum", James Law: Master, out of Londonderry.
The "Dolphin", John Mackay: Master, out of Dublin.
These ships brought 500-700 immigrants to Boston; where most of them wintered among, or more likely, near a Puritan people whose welcome at best was grudging. Some of them went to Casco Bay, near the present town of Portland, where they endured a winter of exceptional severity. In the Spring which followed they found good

land in a pleasant valley nearby in New Hampshire and renamed it Londonderry. This was Frontier territory. The others, who had landed with them at Boston but wintered in Maine, joined them in Londonderry. They were now a sizeable community. Being some distance from the Boston Puritans, they built their own church and a house for their minister, and by 1729 founded four schools in their township. They were a fast breeding lot and by 1780 built ten settlements in New Hampshire and two in Nova Scotia.

Boston and other towns in New England showed in many ways a strong dislike for the Scotch Irish. The differences could hardly have been theological, for who could possibly define beyond reasonable doubt how a Calvinist Puritan differed from a Calvinist Presbyterian in matters or worship? The Bostonians inflicted or tried to inflict many of the petty tyrannies on them from which they had fled England: bigotry and intolerance. They were a closed quasi-bourgeois society that did not like newcomers, whom they found to be unclean, unwholesome and disgusting: a most unChristian attitude. Both sects were British citizens and the Bostonians were probably breaking English Common Law in turning the Scotch Irish away.

Some of those, a sizeable number of families, who landed at Boston went to the frontier township at Worcester. They were welcomed warmly, and acquitted themselves well. Things changed when Bostonian prejudice reared its ugly head in religious matters. The Presbyterians lost their first minister and were encouraged to worship with the Puritans, abandoning their own church, on the understanding that from time to time one of their own would occupy the Puritan pulpit. The Puritans reneged on this agreement and the Presbyterians found themselves paying tithes for a minister not of their choice. They built a new church, which the Puritan majority destroyed. In a very Ulster way they left the area to move west to the frontier to build settlements at Pelham and Coleraine, 40 miles from Worcester. Also at Blandford and in Otsego County in New York state. A Nineteenth Century wit said of Boston, "Where Lowells speak only to Cabots, and Cabots speak only to God."

New York was looked at by some pioneers of the Great Migration, but found it wanting on several fronts. The country areas along the

Hudson River were taken up by large estates, and the authorities had shown no enthusiasm in encouraging Ulster people to settle; land was not cheap. New York thought to possess liberal leanings was strongly under Anglican influence and in the Seventeenth Century had been hard on dissenters. There were only three settlements of Presbyterians in the Eighteenth Century; and where only hundreds came to New York, thousands went to Pennsylvania, Virginia and the Carolinas. German immigrants on the other hand seem to have been more welcome; though later in the Eighteenth Century, skilled men from Ulster increased in number.

New Jersey, not that far from New York, became a famous stronghold of Presbyterianism, though of the Scottish variety, and many made their homes there. It became, despite the absence of Scotch Irish, a very important place for them, because the Presbyterian Church, seeing the need of trained and educated ministers of which the country was desperately short, founded in 1746 Princeton University. This was the first of many colleges of excellence which despatched young ministers, mostly in a westerly direction, to provide guidance and succour to the widely scattered Scotch Irish. It was a daunting prospect for young men, or perhaps not so young, to leave the civilised, urban society of Princeton and travel hundreds of miles on horseback to the frontier territory. Many young men of course, who had ambitions, made the reverse journey, from the West to Princeton; for a migrant family thought it a great honour to have a son become a minister. Many of them became circuit ministers, travelling to points where there was no church, carrying all their goods and chattels on horseback, to preach, to baptize and perhaps bury. A hard life, poor pay, dedicated to the service of God.

Dating from the 1570's, the early days of John Knox in Scotland, the Church was set on a well educated leadership, products of Scottish Universities to propagate the faith to an uneducated people. This was the driving force behind Princeton to maintain Knox's high standards little knowing that in the long run they were fighting a losing battle. There would always be a paucity of ministers, owing to the rapid growth in immigrant population; which led inevitably to a lowering of educational, if not religious, standards. Enter the Baptists, who may have been short on education but very, very long on fundamental Old Testament beliefs and hellfire. Not to mention certain exhortations in St Paul's Epistles, which strike horror in modern day liberals.

Maryland was a hotchpotch of a colony. Chesapeake Bay divided it north to south. The Eastern shore was settled by Englishmen not long after Jamestown. They planted tobacco on large estates; imported indentured servants to do the housework, and bought slaves to do the fieldwork. By 1650 many Presbyterians lived there mostly as indentured servants, who, had they wished to farm, would not have had the money to buy land. From being servants they set out to better themselves as tradesmen, merchants and middlemen. Scots also came as servants, and later were admired as illicit traders in tobacco.

The Western shore had many Scotch Irish who came during the last two decades of the Great Migration; also as servants. Soil exhaustion damaged the tobacco farming and thus the economy generally, and the livelihood of the immigrant class. So there was something of a move North and a proliferation of small farms. Many Scotch Irish were at the Bay's head, and quite near where the Delaware River enters the Bay there was Cecil County, Chester and Lancaster Scotch Irish, a positive Presbyterian stronghold. So in quite a small area there were Scotch Irish and English; all Presbyterians, which created a most amicable society of co-religionists and many intermarriages, English immigration had virtually ceased by 1700, but immigration from Ulster, with some from Germany continued.

The South Carolina Tidewater was not much favoured by the Ulstermen as its economy was slave based, and the Anglican Church was strongly entrenched. Those Presbyterians that did come were mostly from Scotland and came as indentured servants. By 1700 there were sufficient dissenters to build their own church; and because the congregation was made up of Presbyterians, Huguenots and New England Puritans, it was agreed the church should be independent of any formal organisation, but ruled by elders.

Those Scotch Irish who had no interest in farming or Indian fighting saw no reason to arrive in Delaware Bay made their way to Pennsylvania, then West, by way of the Susquehanna and the Shenandoah Valley, sailing direct to Charleston where in various towns on the Tidewater such as Williamsburg, became servants, tradesmen and skilled artisans. Later, on being offered generous terms many moved up country as farmers. Immigration to all intents and purposes stopped at the beginning of the War of Independence. Growth from that point onwards grew by natural increase.

Georgia as far as there is evidence was not seriously considered as a home by immigrants, which is why it was the last of the thirteen colonies to be founded. The English came in 1733, but hardly as immigrants, more as colonials. Colonel Oglethorpe, a British military engineer, started in 1734 to construct 24 elegant squares in a town to be called Savannah, which today is considered to be one of, if not the most, elegant city in the South; very laid back. Sensibly when General William Tecumseh Sherman reached there on his Atlanta to the Sea campaign of slash and burn, the good people, that is, the wealthy held up their hands and said "We surrender." Visitors to that lovely city today should warm to such a response of enlightened self-interest.

Savannah apart, there was little in Georgia except a few settlers, and sporadic fighting with Spaniards and Indians in neighbouring Florida. The English sent convicts there to a penal settlement, and a plantation culture based on slavery developed to a high degree. The first non-English settlers were Scots; as in South Carolina and Maryland the Scotch Irish were slow to come because of the alien nature of slavery. After 1812 when the colonies trustees surrendered the colony to the Crown, the population was still only 2,400. In stable conditions Savannah built itself into a flourishing port, and in the 10 years before the Revolutionary War, the Scotch Irish, having first settled the Carolina Piedmont, crossed the upper Savannah River to establish small farms in the back country. In the 1790 census, Georgia had 82,000 people of whom 52,000 were white; and ninety percent of these lived away from the coast and its slavery in Oglethorpe's original town and settlement.

Frontier life. A strange paradox is bound up in the symbiosis that chained the settler to the Indian. Hating each other perhaps, giving each other horrific nightmares no doubt, did they depend on each other? The Scotch Irish were accustomed to harsh living and short rations and war, but nothing equal to life on virgin land in America, on to which with foolhardy courage they staked their claim. Under constant threat of Indian attack, they learned Indian ways. How to clear a forest; hunting for food; Indian lore of native plants for medicinal purposes. Oats and barley they learned how to plant and crop: Indian corn, such a prolific crop, and pumpkins, squash, beans and sweet potatoes became a part of the planters diet. He was inclined to mimic Indian dress: more practical than white man's clothes; deerskin shirts, moccasins and dressing his hair long. And what did the white man pass on? Well, there was whiskey, guns and diseases against which the Indian had scant immunity.

The laborious work, the long day, made the frontier family appreciate such time off as came their way. Funerals and weddings, both plentiful, were the backbone of relaxation; fuelled by corn whisky (now called whiskey), a delightful bi-product of the corncob. Competitions of all sorts, running, jumping and a brutal form of boxing-cum-wrestling took the tension out of the young before everybody settled down to dancing, singing and drinking, especially drinking, in the evening. The minister of course joined in. Weddings and funerals were always a good time to settle old family disputes, imagined slights and money owed. More fighting, more drinking added to the gaiety of a long, thoroughly enjoyable day.

Such goings-on were an import from Ulster, Scotland and England. The only difference was the drink, at least for the Ulster people. The illicit still had been a feature of Irish life for centuries. When the potato appeared, the stills in the mountains of Donegal used them to distil poteen, a most excellent drink when well made. The English Excise men were at their wits end, trying to find illicit stills, which were highly mobile. Plenty of lookouts, usually children, were able to warn the operators of an approaching Government Excise man. In America, whiskey became a very marketable product, cheap to make, easily transported, with in due course an unexpected customer, the Indian. Corn was a staple diet of the Indian, but he never stumbled on its interesting by-product, alcohol. Nothing changes; all over modern Ireland the principal guest at a funeral wake is not the corpse but the whiskey.

Among the immigrants a man might marry early, and no member of a large family (for the children came quickly) was more important than the wife. She worked as hard as the man; and a bachelor would have found it impossible to survive with even a veneer of civilised behaviour, without a wife to run his house. Only in the fields

The Rifle

The Pennsylvania (née Kentucky) rifle was available in North America from about 1730. It was a locally made version of the hunting rifles, which had been made almost from the beginning of the 18th century, mostly in Austria and Southern Germany. Light to carry and because of the rifling, accurate for the period. Made initially by German and Austrian gunsmiths, they were sold as hunting guns to fill the pot. It was natural that it became the standard and very effective weapon of the American irregulars in the Revolutionary War. Fired from behind tree trunks into close ranks of British Redcoats and well outside the range of the British infantry Brown Bess musket it was deadly. The Brown Bess was designed for short-range use, firing into a close mass of enemy infantry perhaps only fifty yards away. In European warfare it was considered unmanly, unchivalrous to hide behind trees or fire from a distance.

The British finally got the idea, but too late. A British officer of Scottish descent, Patrick Ferguson, invented a breach-loading rifle, patented in 1776. It fired 7 shots a minute and was accurate well beyond 400 yards. He brought it to America, armed a corps of Loyalists, and his rifle was the principal cause of the defeat of the rebels at Brandy Wine in 1777. The British lost 500 men, the rebels 1,000. On 7th October 1780, Major Ferguson fell defending King's Mountain in South Carolina. He was the only Englishman in the battle; all the others were Americans; rebels or loyalists. With Ferguson dead, the impetus for a new infantry gun died until 1790. Probably a pigheaded British Command preferred faithful old Brown Bess, even if the American rebels were unsporting enough to hide behind trees to shoot and scoot.

would a man not want his wife to work. That, in the eyes of an expanding community was the mark of the lower class, and any man, especially if he had some education, expected to be socially mobile among his peers. A brick or stone house to replace the log cabin, more land, employ a hand or two, educate the children and so on.

Whether the settler's early days of struggle were in Pennsylvania, Virginia, the Carolinas or New England, the experience was common to all. It was a fight for survival. So the following details of pioneering vicissitudes in New Hampshire as quoted by James Leyburn in his chapter on frontier society can be taken as typical.

They frequently lie out in the woods several days or weeks together in all seasons of the year. A hut composed of poles and bark, suffice them for shelter; and on the open side of it, a large fire secures them from the severity of the weather. Wrapt in a blanket with their feet near the fire, they pass the longest and coldest nights, and awake vigorous for labour the succeeding day. Their food ...... is salted pork or beef, with potatoes and bread of Indian corn; and their drink is water mixed with ginger: though many of them are fond of distilled spirits. ...Those who begin a new settlement, live at first in a style not less simple. They erect a square building of poles [that is a log cabin] notched at the ends to keep them fast together. The crevices are plaistered with clay or the stiffest earth which can be had, mixed with moss or straw. The roof is either bark or split boards. The chimney a pile of stones; within which a fire is made on the ground, and a hole is left in the roof for the smoke to pass out. Another hole is made in the side of the house for a window, which is occasionally closed with a wooden shutter. In winter, a constant fire is kept, by night as well as by day; and in summer it is necessary to have a continual smoke on account of the musquetos and other insects with which the woods abound. The same defence is used for the cattle; smokes of leaves and brush are made in the pastures where they feed by day, and in the pens where they are folded by night. Ovens are built at a small distance from the houses, of the best stones which can be found, cemented and plaistered with clay or still earth. Many of these first essays in housekeeping, are to be met with in the new plantations, which serve to lodge whole families, till their industry can furnish them with materials, for a more regular and comfortable house; and till their land is so well cleared as that a proper situation for it can be chosen. By these methods of living, the coarse food and hard lodgings; and to be without shoes in all seasons of the year is scarcely accounted a want. By such hard fare, and the labour which accompanies it, many young men have raised up families, and in a few years have acquired property sufficient to render themselves independent freeholders; and they feel all the pride and importance which arise from a consciousness of having well earned their estates.

Wayland Dunaway (Scotch Irish of Colonial Pennsylvania p. 189) justly says "On some towering mountain peak in Pennsylvania, the Commonwealth should erect to the Scotch Irish woman, a monument as a worthy memorial of her character and deeds."

14. How America Democraticised Religion

Isaac Newton, English mathematician and physicist, born in the Seventeenth Century, the greatest single influence on theoretical physics until Albert Einstein, said modestly "If I have seen further it is by standing on the shoulders of giants." It could be said also of Francis Makemie, William Tennant and George Whitefield, that they stood on the shoulders of giants – St Paul, Martin Luther, John Calvin and John Knox – as they evangelised in America, and reduced Christianity to a simple, easily understood belief in God. They were the sowers whose seed fell on fertile ground, and grew mightily right up to present day.

Francis Makemie was an Ulsterman from Laggan. In the light of the name controversy that was to follow, it is interesting to note that Glasgow University recorded the admittance of a young man from Ulster, Francis Makemie, in 1675, describing him as "Scoto Hibernicus", that is Scotch Irish; and he was only one of numerous young men from Ulster wishing to take holy orders by attending a Scottish University, the route to religious preferment in the Presbyterian Church through the Seventeenth and Eighteenth Centuries.

He went to America in 1683 as an ordained minister of the Presbytery of Laggan and founded five churches in Maryland. Not the first minister to arrive on the Eastern shores of Maryland – two or three others had arrived before 1683 – but the most influential. It did his reputation no harm when later he was arrested in New York in 1706 for preaching without a licence. New York was strongly Anglican, and harsh on dissenters. He persuaded the London Presbyterians to send a few ministers to America with provision for their financial support: This was a great triumph. Under his guidance and persuasion, the first Presbytery in America was created at Philadelphia in 1706 by seven ministers from Pennsylvania, Delaware and Maryland. This led to the formation of the first Synod in 1717, composed of the Presbyteries of Long Island, New Castle, Philadelphia and Maryland's Snow Hill. Thus was formed the framework and stable structure within which the Presbyterian Church was to flourish in America, though not without many trials and tribulations. Makemie died in 1708 having given 25 years of his life in selfless service to the church.

William Tennant's background was not dissimilar to Makemie's. A minister from Ulster, a graduate of Edinburgh University, a fine scholar of Latin, Greek and theology; and unusual for a Presbyterian, a more than passing interest in science and the arts. It could be argued that Tennant's contribution to the church's growth was greater than Makemie's for he inherited Knox's zeal for education as central to the church's future. He later evangelised and persuaded communities to establish their own church in the manner one could say of Paul in Corinth, Galatia and Thessalonica. But Tennant's contribution was strategic rather than tactical. He saw the future lay with training young men to become ministers to a high level of learning, particularly in theology, without which the churches would lack discipline. The history of the church, at least since the beginning of the Ulster Plantation in 1610 had shown that the settlers needed ministers to structure their lives, religiously and morally. So when in 1726 he started a school of higher learning at his manse in Neshaminy, Eastern Pennsylvania, he was in fact establishing a seminary for novice priests, though not of the Catholic variety. It was in a cabin attached to the manse, and was spoken of disparagingly as the Log College. He taught in his spare time, and his teaching was rigorous. His pupils were young Scotch Irish boys, and in time a steady stream of ministers graduated from Log College. It was the forerunner of such famous seats of Presbyterian learning as Princeton, founded in 1746 and the other 48 permanent colleges (out of a total of 207) founded in America before the Civil War. If you add to these the 80 others started by Methodists, Congregationalists and Baptists, the contribution of the dissenting religions to American literacy is remarkable.

George Whitefield, the third of this outstanding trio ,was beyond doubt the greater Evangelist; and he was neither Scot, Scotch Irish or Presbyterian. He was a Calvinist, who put even John Wesley's stirring preaching into the shade. Born in 1714, dead at 56 and in that short life made seven visits to America as an Evangelist. No Presbyterian, but his influence on that stern unforgiving church was profound. An Englishman from Liverpool, ordained clergyman of the Church of England, and a friend of the Wesley brothers; like them, he was angry with the Church of England, and its increasing separation from the common people through carelessness and neglect. He wanted to change the church radically. Unlike Wesley who only wanted it to be nicer, more sincerely religious, Whitefield wanted to change it root and branch, and start if necessary a new sect of the Christian religion, which he did. This, Wesley did not want to do; he only wanted the church to change, Just as Paul had no intention of starting a new religion, – he only wanted Judaism to bring itself up to date. Abraham and Moses had played their parts; Judaism should start looking to Jesus Christ, the risen Son of God – Wesley devoutly wished to remain in communion with the Anglican Church.

John Wesley is correctly perceived to be the Father of Methodism in the British Isles, though not in America. He went there as a missionary in 1735 but returned to England in 1738, seemingly having upset the colonials in Savannah where he had an unfortunate love affair with a Miss Hopkey. Meanwhile Whitefield followed Wesley to America in 1738, and broke absolutely with the Anglican Church. Perhaps he could best be described as a Methodist with attitude.

His first visit was to Georgia, and from there he travelled to New England. An Oxford scholar, he preached to the people with uncompromising simplicity. He spoke to the heart, not the mind, and the effect was dramatic. This was the Great Awakening which swept the Colonies, all thirteen of them. Whitefield had no taboos; he had no compunction about offending good taste in the eyes of the educated classes. He addressed, as did Wesley, huge open air meetings, and could have said as Paul did to the Galatians (3:28) "There is neither Jew nor Greek, there is neither bond nor free; there is neither male nor female, master nor slave, for you are all one in Christ Jesus."

His straight from the shoulder speaking injected the staid burghers of Boston, Philadelphia and the settlers of the frontier with paroxysms of pure joy, and it caused great uneasiness in the Presbyteries of the Presbyterian Church. Most serious of all it opened the door to the Methodists and Baptists to poach members from the other sects. In particular the Anglicans, which they did rapidly, and in large numbers. No longer did a young man need to study for 3 years to master Latin, Greek and theology, while immigrants were arriving weekly by the boatload to find their communities bereft of ministers to give them religious succour and comfort. The need for such ministers had been destroyed, almost at a stroke. Such need had been pre-empted by the availability of many robust self-taught laymen, students of the Bible among the settlers' communities. They knew the Bible by heart, the Catechisms Long and Short, the splendid stories both from the Old Testament and the New. They could speak of Hell with confidence in its existence, and of Heaven which awaited those who could, by living the pure life of believing in Jesus and avoid being consigned to Hell. These rustic pastors, mostly unlettered, some illiterate, so captured the confidence of the people that bv 1776 the Baptists had 12% of the population to the Presbyterians 10%; and the Congregationalists which included massive numbers of Methodists 35%.

To the Baptist the gospels were simple, uncomplicated, true and would brook no argument. For how can you argue with the truth? No complex organisation was required. The approval of no Presbytery was unnecessary. Any like minded Christian group could form a church and appoint as their pastor any dedicated Baptist who had received the "call" and could speak the demotic language. No bishops, no hierarchy to discipline religious ardour or correct the theology. If the *amour propre* of the established Faiths was ruffled by the unpolished and sometimes uncouth rantings of the zealots; if the immersions, the baptisms, were unseemly and over emotional, the deep, clear as crystal, belief of the pastor was more important than any lapse of good taste.

When the Great Migration started in 1717 of the many forces urging the Ulster settlers to the ships and the high seas, religious liberty which they considered was being curtailed, if not denied was one of the strongest. The Calvinist Presbyterians decided it was time to go. It fired their departure and sustained them against the hardships of the new country. Some ministers were among the early groups, adequate for attending the wants of the few. But when the tidal wave of the 1725-29 immigrants hit the beaches it left most of the settlers without a minister; and he was missed, sorely missed. The guiding hand that gave confidence to face bereavements and the harshness of work, and perhaps Indian raids gave rise to drunkenness, lack of care for the family, disregard of the law of which there was little enough anyway; and an excess of that curse of the Ulsterman, rugged individuality to do as he damned well pleased.

When the minister lived within his flock, the community rules were strict and few disregarded them. Not only did the minister come down on the miscreant like a ton of bricks, but congregational members also. Paradoxically, the strictness made everybody feel safe. Respecting the minister made his rules theirs also, and there was no other way to live. Sunday was a day of absolute religious observance: as strict as a Jewish Sabbath. Work ceased, private and public prayer was solemnly observed. It was not unusual for Sunday worship to last almost from sunrise to sunset. It might sound boring to those of little faith, but in fact it was such a release from six days of labouring, for women as well as men, the children also played a part. Sunday was a day to be joyfully anticipated: Work ceased on Saturday night, then private family prayers were followed by public prayers conducted by the minister. Tedious perhaps to a modern congregation but not to an Eighteenth Century gathering. It was listened to carefully and remembered for discussion in the week ahead. If the preacher held his audience; a bit of an actor perhaps, it was the high point in a day of devout worship. The people got to know the minister best from his sermons. Wearisome sometimes, but also discursive with the whole of the Bible on which to draw. An opening talk, the expanding of the subject point by point, and a thundering finale, like the end of a Beethoven symphony. It could have all the excitement of a good play (though no right thinking minister would ever have gone to a theatre).

Such a sermon would be typical of one given in Scotland at the time of John Knox or to the settlers in Ulster during the Plantation; and it was what the Scotch Irish immigrants wanted. Only a Presbyterian Minister could fulfil this need, and without him the community would start to lose cohesion. In the settled towns of Philadelphia, and many others in the Middle Colonies, Church attendance was regular, a bit automatic perhaps, and the enthusiasm was frequently less than that expected from followers of Knox. The Sabbath was kept, and rather according to the law than the spirit. The edge of vigorous devotion had been lost. The ministers were comfortable in their brick built manses, and the stipend, if not over generous, always arrived. In short, they were stuck in their ways with minds firmly closed to change. Worst of all they were not much concerned about their brethren, now numbered in many thousands on the dangerous frontiers of Pennsylvania, Virginia and the Carolinas. Out of sight, out of mind.

So, when in the 1730s educated young ministers started to arrive, graduates of the four Scottish Universities – Glasgow, Edinburgh, St Andrew's and Aberdeen – no less devout than their forbears, but full of new ideas, it came as a shock. New ideas of how to serve the faithful and bringing the Godless, the slipshod and the timeservers back into the fold. And how did they intend to do it? By taking the Church to the people, not waiting for the people to come to the church. This new breed of minister was called New Siders, as opposed to Old Siders, who neither liked nor trusted the changes put forward by these intellectual intruders; Presbyterians though they may be. The Old Siders had only contempt for the likes of George Whitefield, and by 1745 a schism had developed in the church. Shades of Paul and the Nazarenes after the Crucifixion. The Old Siders did not think religion should be easy, nor should it be made easier for the common people. This was precisely the argument between the Jewish Establishment, the Sanhedrin in Jerusalem and Paul; and many Presbyterians as with the other faiths started to listen to Whitefield the Methodist.

Before Whitefield the shortage of ministers had been recognised, and William Tennant's Log College welcomed. There followed Princeton, Hampden-Sydney, Samuel Blair's at Fagg's Manor, Newark Academy and others. The idea was to reduce dependency on university trained ministers from outside America. The idea was sound but insufficient to deal with the sheer numbers of the Presbyterian immigrants, which by 1776 had reached 200,000. The need had been too great even by the 1730s to be satisfied by home-grown ministers; and the arrival of Whitefield came just in time. It might be said, that if he had not come, it would have been necessary to have invented him. He made God's love a reality; the existence of sin beyond doubt; the thought of hell unbearable, and Heaven attainable. To him the condition of a man's soul was paramount, exceeding all other considerations.

The Schism was closed in 1758, by the Old Siders and New Siders reaching agreement without victory being claimed by either. Both sides agreed that somehow funds and suitable educational facilities *must* be provided to train enough ministers for the swollen population. But it was too late, the dam was holed.

Not only the Presbyterian Church lost members to the Baptists;every faith without exception contributed to the growth of the Baptist and Methodist Chapels. Despite the changing face of religion in America, the Presbyterian Church clung strongly to its beliefs and structure of the Church, the Presbytery and the Synod and never lowered the educational standards required of its ministers.

After Independence the Appalachians were crossed and the Ohio Valley occupied by settlers. Whitefield had been dead since 1770, but his meetings, the forerunners of the "revivalist meeting", were seized on avidly by both Methodists and Baptists. The two sects, but particularly the Baptists, were evangelists to a level that never let the truth get in the way of a good story. They were rigorous and vigorous in selling the word of God in a way that no Protestant, indeed, any Christian had encountered before; and it worked.

The loss of some members, indeed many members wounded the Presbyterian Church, but far from fatally; the majority was strengthened by the defection of the weaklings; and by 1790 it no longer looked to Scotland or England for leadership; it was now Americanised. The Church had become what it was to remain for more than a century, a denomination of strict people of steady character and seriously theological. It did not encourage revivals, it esteemed both social and self-discipline, and membership of the middle class. It did not bow to Unitarianism and held on tightly to much that it had brought from Ulster.

15. Scotch Irish in Politics

When a people makes significant contributions to the well-being of a nation, in such fields as politics, science, business and warfare, it would be surprising if, from time to time, a myth or two did not get attached to the truth and end up as historical fact. Especially when the people in question were but a small part of the nation's population. In this the Scotch Irish were doing no more than following tradition.

The Presbyterian settlers came to America from the province of Ulster in Ireland as political innocents. No local, no national experience in running affairs. They were not given the opportunity to do such public duties; only in family matters could they be said to have experience. After the Battle of the Boyne in 1690 they were not represented in the Dublin Irish Parliament. The Test Act passed by the British Parliament in London in 1703, though aimed at the Catholics rather than Dissenters, was turned in Dublin by chicanery and bias into a tool to keep Presbyterians and other dissenters in their place. That is, in a permanently subordinate state. Such action by European Governments of the times was not unusual. A government's religion was the State Religion, which did not tolerate minor sects. Such a policy started in AD324 when Constantine the Great made Christianity the State Religion of the Romans; and he said "I will make Christianity the footstool of my Empire." From that time until the Test Act of 1703 and beyond in *all* Christian Kingdoms, the State Religion became the tool of the State; or worse, the personal property of the Monarch. So the Anglican Irish Parliament meant nothing personal when robbing Dissenting Churches of authority. The Presbyterian Church did not see it that way.

The Act was passed by Parliament, but it was the Anglican Church that called the tune, both in England, Wales and Ireland; but not in Scotland where the Covenanters, by battles against England, won the right to their own Established Church, the Church of Scotland, which was of course Presbyterian. Proscriptions were taken against *all* Dissenters of such severity as had never been encountered by the settlers of the Plantation since they first arrived in 1610.

They included:

Ministers were turned out of their pulpits, or threatened with the Law.

People in some parts of Ulster were not permitted to bury their dead unless an Anglican clergyman was present to conduct the burial service.

With no official standing ministers could not conduct marriages. If they did, the marriage was declared illegal; and children of the illicit ceremony, bastards.

If Dissenters did not take communion in an Anglican Church or accept the Thirty Nine Articles of the Book of Common Prayer, then all positions, civil and military were denied to them.

Children could not be taught by Dissenters.

There were other equally demeaning actions enacted against Dissenters. In England, the Test Act was not severely applied; but in Ireland it was devastating. In Belfast the whole corporation of administration was dismissed; in Londonderry ten out of twelve aldermen. Among migrants to America nobody can remember a single lawyer, judge or politician as the Test Act continued until 1782. A complete population reached America between 1717 and 1775, of which barely a handful had any knowledge of how to run a village, much less a town. Yet of the various skills attributed to the Scotch Irish, politics ranked high. How could this be? It was not in the blood or the genes; where did it come from? The Presbyterian Church, of course: its structure, and its highly educated ministers. Alas, few came with the migrants in the early days, and never enough even as late as 1775; but wherever they were, the democratic structure of the Church played a large part in turning its congregations and communities into ordered, organised and law abiding townships. For the times, the Presbyterian Church was loosely democratic. It elected its officials locally. There was a federation of independent Presbyteries, and each Presbytery elected the people to represent it in the General Assembly. Each congregation could choose its own minister, which they had been able to do in Ulster before the Test Act. By comparison with the Anglican or Puritan Churches it was admirably democratic. The minister was the key; without him there was chaos, and the further the pioneers pushed West, the greater was the need of ministers but the fewer there were. Nevertheless as time went by enough ministers were at hand to provide a useful level of democracy among the Scotch Irish.

In America, especially after the War of Independence, there arose the endearing legend that the Constitutional Convention of 1787 decided that the organisation of the Presbyterian Church offered a ready-made system of how the Government of the United States of America should function. ,In fact there were few Presbyterians at the Convention, and even fewer Scotch Irish according to the records. But the fact that the legend gained currency, and that many Scotch Irish believed it, indicates how quickly this influential sector of the immigrant population had grown politically, and would continue to do so for the next 100 years or more.

Taking an American rather than a European view, the Scotch Irish were healthy democrats. They believed a government required the consent of the governed both at local and national levels. But there were caveats. They were not always willing to submit to established institutions if it was thought not to be in their interests. This irritated democratically elected officials greatly, although history frequently shows that a mere handful of radical objectors can so influence a government as to cause it to change a fundamental policy. It was only a minority of rebels that precipitated the rebellion against the British Crown. The War of Independence was well advanced before anything like a majority of the American people was prepared to resist British Rule root and branch. Those rebels should have remembered that when they looked with distaste on Scotch Irish agitation. The Loyalist, or Tories as the rebels called them were never less than 20% of the people, and for a long time at least a third. New York to the very end had a loyalist majority.

In the early days of the Great Migration, the mass of Scotch Irish could not have spelt "political action" much less practice it. They saw no need to. If they had land, however acquired, tools to clear it and seed to sow that, for the moment, was enough. Only when those acquisitions were put in danger from taxes, tithes and Indians, did they appreciate that, unlike in Ulster, they had the chance to oppose those who were the proponents of their woes and get something done. When finally they were the largest immigration population in Pennsylvania, Virginia, the Carolinas and even Georgia, it is not surprising that it was there that the Scotch Irish emerged kicking and screaming into public life. There was nothing in their Ulster background to prepare them to achieve skills in fighting Indians or taking a leading role in politics, local, national or colonial, but when the need came they took to them as to the manner born.

James Logan, Secretary to the Pennsylvania Assembly and himself an Ulsterman, though a Quaker was prophetic when, in 1729 he gloomily said: "The common fear is that, if they thus continue to come, they will make themselves proprietors of the Province. It is strange that they thus crowd where they are not wanted. The Indians themselves are alarmed at the swarms of strangers, and we are afraid of a breach between them; for the Irish are very rough to them." It was another 35 years before they started to be rough intruders into Pennsylvania Quaker-controlled politics.

The instrument of change could not have been more surprising when it turned out to be the Paxton Boys who butchered the Conestoga Indians after Pontiac's War in December 1763. Outraged that the Quakers seemed more prepared to protect the Indians from the settlers than afford the settlers on the frontier help and protection from the Indians, the angry Scotch Irish drew up a "Remonstrance" in 1766 and sent a delegation, or rather a small army, of 500 men to Philadelphia, Remonstrance in hand. It was not an orderly meeting, more a mob threatening an authority losing its dignity by the minute. The Protest within the Remonstrance covered many things, but the one concerned with the current inequality of representation was beyond argument. Pennsylvania at that time had eight counties. The three Eastern counties around Philadelphia sent 26 members to the Assembly; the remaining ten were sent by the five counties in the West of the state. The emerging debating skill of the angry settlers was shown when with astounding cheek, they quoted the English Crown in their support. "We apprehend that as free men and English subjects we have an indisputable title to the same privileges and immunities with his Majesty's other subjects, who reside in the interior counties of Philadelphia, Chester and Bucks, and therefore ought not to be excluded from an equal share with them in the very important privilege of legislation." Such arguments won the Scotch Irish many allies among the rest of the population.

How ironical, that at the same time, the colonial authority at Williamsburg Virginia, a future centre of loyalist activity, was very sympathetic to the settlers on the frontier. They listened sensibly, understood the problem and gave help in the defence of the frontier. When Indian attacks multiplied, no other colony was more active than Virginia in aiding the settlers in their dangerous task. Other help came from the Established Church of England; most unexpected. The Scotch Irish, pragmatic when necessary, and working on the historical precept "Our enemy's enemy is our friend" were grateful and took part in the splendid parish organisation at a local level which the Church had brought from England, with its large measure of self-government. The parish was a division of the county, and the Church laid down the basis of local taxes, and appointed Justices of the Peace as established in England since the Fourteenth Century; and the churchwardens looked after the village poor and orphans. Religious toleration was allowed in Virginia, and the settlers appointed their own vestrymen, churchwardens, and obtained valuable experience in running their affairs protected by the British Crown.

They were not so lucky in North Carolina where the easterners on the Tidewater had a low opinion of back country settlers, and had no intention of granting them any degree of self-government. They were ignorant rubbish and must be satisfied with whatever was allowed them. In short, politics in North Carolina was dominated by the Plantocracy with the same iniquities so common in Pennsylvania. Coastal counties each had five members in the Legislature while inland counties had only two. There were murmurings from the settlers from 1759. Then serious trouble started, caused by disproportionate taxes, crooked lawyers and judges, abuse of land laws and religious intolerance. Some angry settlers started a movement called the "Regulation" to take action outside the law if redress could not be reached peacefully. Months of violence followed, threats and discord broke up local government. Governor Tyron sent in troops to settle the business by force – at a cost. The Regulators were defeated, fifteen ringleaders hanged, after what has gone down in North Carolina history as the Battle of Alomance, 16th May 1771.

The Scotch Irish emerged as usual from such conflict as heroes or villains. Heroes, because they were prepared to face the county's well-armed militia, ready to die if necessary. Villains, because they took the law into their own hands, and killed state representatives. Two thousand Regulators, poorly armed and poorly led, were defeated in open battle by one thousand trained and well-armed soldiers who lost nine dead with sixty-nine wounded. The Regulators losses were considerable but unrecorded.

Time and time again there were serious and dangerous incidents involving the Scotch Irish who were not prepared to accept established law if they considered the law to be unjust – to them. The Paxton Boys were the first to cause serious rioting and killings to achieve, in their view, justice. The Battle of Alomance was followed by other incidents in South Carolina, triggered generally by the Scotch Irish's well honed sense of injustice. They were involved in one affray after another.

The Whiskey Rebellion of 1794

The English never sent more than a handful of Excise men to the wild hills of Donegal to apprehend a few illicit makers of poteen, the powerful distillation of the humble potato. The Scotch Irish, even for them, excelled in their recognised opposition to established order when they took on the Government of the United States; refusing to pay the 25% tax levied on alcohol sales. The tax was necessary (one supposes) to pay for the Revolutionary War. The Farmers, (for they were no longer settlers) of Western Pennsylvania tarred and feathered the tax collectors. Local officials were ordered to arrest the leaders of the revolt, which enraged them even more. The commander of the local militia, James McFarlane, was shot dead as he defended a besieged tax collector, John Neville. The Farmers objected to the tax as an unfair attack on their livelihood. Whiskey was interesting, as it was value added to the corn crop. It was as certain as night follows day that the Scotch Irish would distil whiskey from it, in the absence of potatoes. After all, they were Irish. The transport of high value whiskey was also much less than bulky low value corn.

The rebellion was easily put down. The Government, not one to do things by halves, not only sent an army of 12,000 to break the whiskey distillers, but the President of the United States himself no less had put on his chief rebel's uniform of the American Revolutionary Army, to lead it. The expression "Crushing a butterfly with a steam hammer" comes to mind. I wonder if the irony occurred to George as he, the leading rebel, was sent to punish fellow rebels whom he had once regarded as the backbone of his rebel army. The tax was unpopular nationwide, and the farmers considered they had sound moral justification. However, not for the first time the Scotch Irish, illegal, rough and ready, self-righteous, bloody-minded Ulster attitude had a good result. As the 40th President, Ronald Regan often said "There you go again."

Thomas Jefferson resigned his position as Secretary of State in protest of the tax, and went on to help form the Democratic Republican Party which supported states' rights against the power of the Federal Government. Alexander Hamilton, Secretary to the Treasury, who had imposed the tax, resigned; and partly because of the Whiskey Rebellion, the Federalist Party in Washington broke up.

Secretary James Logan, 50 years earlier, might have thought, in a moment of gloom, "Why can't these Ulstermen behave like the peace loving Germans? They always do as they are told."

They learned the street fighting end of politics; which, in the fullness of time, when they had attained respectability, served them well in the body politic of America.

Looking at the overall effect of the advent of the Ulstermen on to the American continent, it seems to have been one of unending struggle. Firstly, to obtain a foothold of land on which they could farm, and raise a family. Secondly, to live according to and under the guidance of the Presbyterian Church; and thirdly, to play a role in the establishing of democracy in America. Not, at least in the early days, appearing overly concerned with politics, they tumbled into the political maelstrom almost by accident. Most likely they found they had a talent for it. They wanted land; the state authorities were slow to act so they took it. Their confiscation of Indian land, owned by the natural law of possession led to cruel war on both sides. Firstly, unaided by the authorities, and then grudgingly, as the settlers made themselves a veritable threat to the governments of the Middle and Southern States. The authorities were bewildered by these strange Calvinistic Irish who considered God and natural justice to be undeniably on their side. Such conduct had never been seen elsewhere in America. Not in Puritan New England: certainly not in the Tidewater territory of North and South Carolina. *Never* among the huge immigrant population of Germans. Within this 50 years or so of strife and struggle, finally wherever they were in a majority they imposed their authority for better or for worse. Gradually, the Crown, Governors and officials in general came to accept the status quo established by the settlers, whose influence and authority grew to maturity.

It is interesting to regard the list of Presidents to the Congress from 1774 to 1789. The First was Peyton Roundolph from Virginia; and the last of the sixteen also of Virginia. Nine of those were from states in which the Scotch Irish were probably a majority from Pennsylvania West and South to Virginia, the Carolinas, Delaware and Maryland. The population of the thirteen states in the census of 1790 is given as 3,172,444. Various attempts have been made to determine the Scotch Irish element. From 6% to 16% say some. The figure of 14% is thought to be most accurate, (or should we say least inaccurate) which gives a population of 454,000. One can only guess how many of them voted in 9 out of 16 Presidents of Congress in that period.

The claim that Scotch Irish stock contributed many political leaders to American public life is easily defended. Descendants of the original Ulster immigrants from Andrew Jackson, the seventh President and sixteen other Presidents have graced the White House, with many others in Congress, the Senate, the High Courts and Gubernatorial Mansions. It is sometimes said that this predilection of Scotch Irish for high office in public life owes something to a genetic quality passed on from generation to generation and out of proportion to their numbers. The number of Scots in the current Cabinet of the British Government and also in both Houses of Parliament is astounding.

The population of Scotland is just over five million. England plus Wales has fifty-three million. In Ulster, it is about one-and-three-quarters.

Scotch Irish contribution to American life and prosperity has been rock hard; and the general effect has been rather like that of a battering ram, or heavy artillery on a fortress wall, which in the end collapses under the onslaught of a relentless force. A force though for good, and without it, without that avalanche of determined Celtic Irish Scottish men and women in the Eighteenth Century, American history may have been different.

Freemasonry

The origins of Freemasonry are in late Seventeeth Century Scotland; or at least the modern form of the cult, the craft, or the brotherhood of this Secret Society. But its origins are as hazy as its international Anglo Saxon influence has been great. In 1717, the New Grand Lodge of England brought four lodges together under one authority. Freemasonry has always claimed to have influenced the course of the War of Independence, either on one side or the other or both. The Order of Freemasonry has always been even-handed in such matters. It is beyond reasonable doubt that there were Freemasons among the Plantation settlers, since its origins lay in Lowland Scotland; and it is therefore also likely that some had found their way to America, where a welcome would have awaited them. Some sea captains and people in mercantile affairs were in America as early as 1680.

The Movement was never overtly political, but covertly? Probably when advantageous. It is assumed that six of the first thirteen Presidents were Masons; and historical records include George Washington, Benjamin Franklin, Admiral John Paul Jones (initiated in Scotland), Paul Revere, John Hancock, General Joseph Warren and John Rowe, who inspired the Boston Tea Party. The Movement would have been strongest in Massachusetts, New York, the English upper class families in the Carolina Tidewaters and Virginia. Of the Scotch Irish in the period up to the War of Independence little is known about Masonic membership, but it is on record that Andrew Jackson, the seventh President, was initiated in 1800, James Buchanan, the fifteenth President, was initiated in 1851 and William McKinley, twenty-fifth President, was initiated in 1865. Freemasonry flourished in the Nineteenth and Twentieth Centuries and the Brotherhood included Presidents Theodore Roosevelt, Franklin Roosevelt and Henry Truman, and it would be surprising if there were not others. In Great Britain Freemasonry was always strong in the armed forces, particularly the Royal Navy. The Church of England especially among the Bishops and the higher clergy was fertile ground for the Movement; and most bizarre of all, the British Royal Family; at least from George III's onwards, princelings and royal dukes were numerous among the cult. No wonder Freemasonry was able to influence affairs in Great Britain and the United States of America.

A quotation from "Beginnings of Freemasonry in America Before 1750" by Melvin M Johnson (1924) is revealing. "A study of the Tremendous influence which Freemasonry had in the pre-revolutionary days, in the years of the war throughout the formative period of American institutions, will demonstrate that Freemasonry had exercised a greater influence upon the establishment of American civilisation and the fundamentals of this Government than any other single institution."

16. The Scotch Irish at War

"Who shall write the history of the American Revolution? Who can write it? Who will ever be able to write it?" Thus wrote ex-President John Adams to ex-President Thomas Jefferson on 30th July 1815. To Adams, the Revolution "was a radical change in the principles, opinions, sentiments, and affections of the people; and it began in the minds and hearts of the people."

Those reflections of Adams were wiser than the received wisdom of later generations which avowed that the Revolution was caused by resentment of Britain's commercial policies towards the colonies, and by Americans having no say in political decisions that affected their interests. That view was wildly simplistic. In the minds of the natural leaders of New England, an idea, a certainty, that one day an articulate, experienced, sophisticated people would be granted self-rule as an independent nation was beyond doubt, and there was no alternative. The question was when and how? There were signs and murmurs; such as the Boston Tea Party in May 1773, at which it was believed the smarter raider filled his capacious pockets before hurling the tea chests overboard. There had been the Boston Massacre, when British sentries fired at a jeering mob during a snowball fight in March 1770. Five people were killed, and all but two of the sentries acquitted, by an American court, and the defending lawyer was John Adams, the second President no less. There were other signs also; but the *casus belli* was probably the Battle of Bunker Hill on June 15th 1775. The British, under siege, virtually surrounded by a rebel force, and forced to take military action, broke the siege with much blood spilt on both sides. As General Sir Henry Clinton said "It was a dearly bought victory, another such would have ruined us. It was a battle that should never have been fought, on a hill that should never have been defended." If there had been another fifty British victories, the Revolution would still have triumphed. It was not a Revolution in the pure sense, more a civil war between members of the same family; and civil wars are the worst. Look at the history of the War of 1861, and the Spanish Civil War of 1936.

For the British, uncomfortably, reluctantly, it was a case of "Let loose the dogs of War"; and the longest in American history (until Vietnam) started. Many British statesmen and intellectuals knew it was a war that should never have been started, and one that could never be won. Britain had never had a big army, and there had never been a draft or conscription. The lines of supply and communication were too long. British strength had always been on the open seas and its Navy was about to be stretched to the limit. Moreover, the hearts of the mass of the people were not in the war; neither were many officers and soldiers. It was a civil war, rich in suffering, deceit, treachery and exiles; and for most if not the *whole* of the war at least one in five Americans stayed loyal to George III. It saw the first use of guerrillas; Sir John Moore of later fame in Spain, where he was killed at Corunna, said he had learnt in America the value of the rifle as a skirmishing weapon, and of mobility, all of which his Rifle Brigade put to devastating use against Napoleon. The Virginian and Kentuckian riflemen were described as "The most fatal widow-makers in the world."

The War of American Independence; an ideological as much as an armed war was rich in incidents, in brave and hesitant men, in timidity and treachery. It was from this long and bitter struggle, fought by mercenaries as well as patriots, that a republican government emerged to rule a territory still largely unmapped and so extensive that few thought it could survive united and a republic for long. Another eighty-five years were to pass and a costly civil war between the North and the Confederacy before the Republic could feel secure.

From 1776 the Scotch Irish people proved their worth as true Americans and offered the most stable and resourceful regiments to Washington's Continental Army, and militia fighting on their home ground of the Carolinas. Battles were unorthodox, unlike those in Europe, and were fought in several and separate theatres of operations. – a war of attrition, killing men and destroying crops and materials. Not permanent occupation of territory – the British never had enough men to do that; nor, for that matter, the Americans. The thirteen colonies had two and a quarter millions from which to draw men; the British, even including thirty thousand Hessian mercenaries (of doubtful value as it proved), never mustered more than sixty thousand over the whole eight years of the conflict, even counting the American Loyalists who were in the invidious and extremely dangerous position of divided loyalties.

The British strategy of breaking up the cohesion of the colonies succeeded with the capture and permanent occupation of New York, and Washington's retreat to Pennsylvania, but the Hudson River campaign, owing to bad planning and the brilliant generalship of Benedict Arnold, resulted in the ignominious defeat at Saratoga. The second theatre was in the Carolinas, leading to the capture of Charleston, Savannah, and other coastal towns and the tiring enervating backcountry campaigns leading to the blockade in Yorktown. Outnumbered two to one by Washington by land, and a large French naval force by sea, Cornwallis was forced into capitulation and effectively the end of the campaign in the South. That in a nutshell, may be the story of the American War of Independence.

The first visible signs of Scotch Irish activity in the run-up to war was probably what came to be called the Mecklenburg Declaration of Independence, dated eventually as May 20th 1775, which, the signatories claimed, was the basis of that other Declaration signed in Philadelphia on July 4th 1776. There is no doubt that those who signed the Mecklenburg Declaration were honest men of probity and patriots including, it is said, many Freemasons. Twenty seven signed; and the substance of the Declaration was contained in six resolutions which resembled the same aims in the Declaration of Independence signed in Philadelphia, and had it come to the attention of the Crown Authorities in North Carolina the signatories would have been arrested for treason and probably hanged. The fourth resolution requested that a copy be forwarded to the Continental Congress in session in Philadelphia. It never arrived. Mr McKitt, the secretary, had been requested to make five copies. On April 16th 1800, a fire at his home destroyed all records of the Declaration, including the original. It seems inconceivable that men of such status as the signatories were lying; but certainly the Great and the Good in Philadelphia, in particular Jefferson and Alexander, refused to accept it had ever existed, or the authenticity of any rival Declaration. Moreover, John Adams said that if anything contributed to the inspiration for the American Revolution it was James Otis' 1761 Massachusetts speech. On 12th April 1776 the Provincial Congress of North Carolina instructed its delegates to the Continental Congress "To concur with the delegates of the other colonies in declaring." Virginia, a month later, instructed its delegates to "propose" independence.

Mecklenburg is, of course, a town in North Carolina.

1775: was the year of skirmishes, and the creation of legends. Of Paul Revere and his ride to Concord. The skirmish between the British Red Coats and Rebels at Lexington Green, resulted in 73 British dead and 200 wounded. The American losses were 49 dead and 16 wounded. There was an eleven month siege of Boston and on June 15th the Battle of Bunker Hill, clearly won by the British but at a cost of 1150 dead out of 2500 soldiers engaged. 96 officers were killed; the rebels would have been almost entirely inhabitants of Boston and Massachusetts. There followed a further six months siege of Boston before the British deemed it sensible to abandon the city. They never returned.

1776: The British sailed from Boston on 17th March along with 1000 royalists who and their forebears had lived in Boston for over 100 years. Such is the cruelty of war, way outside the fighting. The destination was New York, which was never to be lost. Washington was in positions around the city, but was driven out in August across the Hudson River, across the Jerseys and the Delaware.

In the previous month the Declaration of Independence was signed on 4th July. Up to 3 days before, both Pennsylvania and South Carolina had opposed it. By mid-December the Rebel Forces were well out of sight and General Sir William Howe, commander of all the British Forces in America, settled down to a comfortable winter in New York with his mistress Mrs Loring. Then suddenly on December 24th, before his militia decided to go home for Christmas, Washington returned over an ice-choked Delaware River in foul conditions, surprised Colonel Rall and his still festive Hessians at Trenton. A great victory: Rall was killed and 1000 prisoners taken. Washington did not lose a single man in action; however, Lieutenant (and future President) James Monroe was wounded, and two men froze to death.

1777: Pursued by Cornwallis a few days later, Washington gave the British another bloody nose at Princeton, causing 300 casualties; then returned to Morristown to settle into winter quarters. A determined British drive might have finished him; he only had 3,000 men, but they left him alone. Howe, realising he had to take the initiative, sailed from New York with 15,000 men, heading for Philadelphia, by the back way. Instead of sailing up the Delaware he said round Cape Charles and up the Chesapeake, baffling Washington's army, which had no idea of the British position. Howe ended at Head Elk in Maryland, 55 miles from Philadelphia, while Washington occupied a place between the city and the enemy.

Washington stationed his troops on Brandywine Creek, which runs parallel to the Schuylkill River. Howe repeated his Long Island tactic of a left hook, which turned Washington's right flank. On 11th September, Brandywine gave Howe a fine victory, losing 500 dead to the American 1000. It also witnessed the success of Major Ferguson and his sharpshooters using his breach loading 6 shots a minute rifle. A series of satisfactory victories in small battles were won by the British at Poeli, Chew House and others, using the bayonet to good effect, against which the Americans were never happy. Washington retired to Valley Forge for an uncomfortable winter, and the British entered Philadelphia to spend a very comfortable one.

Meanwhile, General John Burgoyne, who arrived in Canada on 6th May, set out in June, down the valley of the Hudson with 7,213 men, some Canadian loyalists, an artillery train, 400 unreliable Indians and many women and children – camp followers. Never had he or any other general in America encountered such fearsomely hostile territory. And, if his reconnaissance had been reliable and thorough, he would never had started the campaign. It was a tremendous gamble; he had been promised that a strong British Force would advance North from New York. The two forces would squeeze the rebel force between them, and New England would be cut-off from all action west of the Hudson and the Delaware. By the end of July, Burgoyne had reached the head of the Hudson, having taken 24 days to travel 23 miles. No fighting, just broken bridges, burnt crops, ravines, rocky gorges, felled trees, mosquitoes and heavy rain. As absurd a campaign as ever planned in the long history of the British army. Doomed to failure; starving and dispirited soldiers, starving horses, easy targets for the American sharp-shooters; lightly clad and hiding behind tree trunks; the heroism of Benedict Arnold, the future traitor, and his good leadership triumphed. Burgoyne capitulated at Saratoga on 10th October. Sir Henry Clinton, supposedly coming from the South, never arrived and seemed totally unconcerned. Burgoyne, soldier, parliamentarian and playwright, returned to the lush salons of London.

After Washington crossed the Delaware he gained thousands of Scotch Irish recruits and at Valley Forge in the winter of 77/78, many of them were veterans of the frontier fighting. He found he could depend on them to be valiant soldiers, used to hardship, unlikely to desert or surrender easily.

1778: The Spring brought hope to the Continental Army. A German Prussian officer, Baron Friedrich von Steuben, claiming to have been a general under Frederick the Great, but really only a captain, Welhelm Steube, was appointed drill master. His methods were unorthodox but effective, despite the only English he knew was "Goddam". He instilled discipline, respect for sanitation, and in a few months, created a fighting force out of a rabble. The army became professional.

In February, France had signed a treaty of alliance with Benjamin Franklin in Paris, as the American Plenipotentiary. That information did not reach George Washington until 1st May. What he did not know was that the Secretary to the American Embassy was George Bancroft, who had been a British spy since 1775 and was to remain so throughout the war. In fact, it was 100 years before the American Government learned about this. There was consternation in London at Bancroft's despatches; for with French help, particularly in war material, the chances of final victory became remote. So the British moved out of Philadelphia in June, back to New York, and the Americans moved in as the British moved out. There were no more battles in the North for the rest of the war, only sporadic raids.

In November, Sir Henry Clinton had sent 3500 troops under Lieutenant Colonial Archibald Campbell to Savannah; he landed near the mouth of the river on 23rd December. The composition of the force was representative of British Forces in the South, two battalions of Scottish Highlanders, two Hessian battalions, and four of Loyalists. They easily overcame an American force of 850 regulars and militia, the only Americans in that part of the South. Georgia returned to British allegiance and remained so to well after the end of the war. Benjamin Franklin said that disease in Georgia would defeat the British but it didn't.

1779: The Americans tried to regain Savannah in the September, under Benjamin Lincoln, with 2000 men attacking from the landside while a French Fleet attacked from the sea. Heavy bombardment badly damaged the town, but the joint Franco American attack was ill-planned and failed. 657 French and 457 Americans were killed or wounded and 55 British. The American force included the 2nd South Carolina Regiment and 1st Battalion Charleston militia, both of which contained many Scotch Irish from the Carolinian Piedmont, who had settled there during the Great Immigration Wave of 1740/41. This would have been their first taste of the Southern campaign that would continue to the war's end.

1780: For Washington, '79 had not been good, and after a hard Winter, his command was down to 10,400 on paper, of whom 2,800 were due to complete their term of service in May. By April he only had 4,000 fit for duty, and officers fed on bread and water, saving the meat for the soldiers. There was open mutiny in the Connecticut Line.

By contrast Clinton had 28,500 soldiers of which 10,800 were Hessians and 4,072 Loyalists. Somebody *must* have noticed that Clinton had recruited more Loyalists than Washington had patriots. It begs the question, in terms of the nation, who was a patriot and who a rebel? Clinton now turned to what was to become his southern strategy, and in 90 transports set sale for Charleston on 29th December 1779, with not a French frigate or warship in sight. A bad voyage, many horses and stores lost. One dismasted transport drifted for many weeks until it reached Cornwall, off the English south west coast. It was not until early April that Cornwallis, the British general commanding, was able to attack a heavily defended town and port with General Lincoln in command,

America invades England?

The confidence of Congress was such that early in 1779, they allowed Franklin and Lafayette to plan a hair-brained invasion of England. The alliance of France with Spain, they thought, made it feasible; though Spain refused to ally with the republican Americans. The French Fleet in Brest put to sea for Corunna to rendezvous with the Spanish Fleet. A joint force of 66 ships was to control the English Channel and protect an army of 31,000 to cross from Le Havre and St Malo and land in the area of Portsmouth. Sir Charles Hardy, admiral of the Channel Fleet, had not been to sea for 20 years. Franklin gave John Paul Jones (born in Scotland) clear orders for the invasion (though what competence Franklin had for such overture is anybody's guess), and even clearer instructions to Lafayette, at one point destined to be the overall commander. 22nd March was to be D-day, but the Spanish Fleet was late and slow, the French were too long at sea, their crews sickly, ill-fed, and storms prevailed. By late August Hardy was back at Spithead, Channel Command, and the Franco American advantage lost. They never landed in England with 5,500 men. Lincoln capitulated. It was another nasty war with Colonel Banastre Tarleton ruthless again with his 500 dragoons. 5,000 Americans surrendered, but the butcher's bill could have been worse. It was the biggest American surrender in American history until Bataan in 1942. For the British it was a pointless victory, fought in two widely separated theatres, cut off by a sea link now imperilled by the French; the Royal Navy all too frequently being absent on what was considered more important tasks. Whoever commanded the Atlantic commanded the future. Dispersion meant defeat, as it proved.

Cornwallis moved North towards Camden in which direction 350 Virginian troops under Colonel Abraham Buford were known to be active. They were chased by the infamous Colonel Tarleton, whose cavalry rode over 100 miles in 54 hours, overtaking them at Waxhaws. Only 53 Virginians survived. Tarleton's losses were 5 killed, 14 wounded and his savagery was relentless. On 31st May, Cornwallis entered Camden. It was clear that a phase of nastiness typical of a civil war had been entered. Guerrilla fighting by the Americans was countered by British ruthlessness. Loyalist support was erratic but necessary, and Tarleton found Mecklenburg and Rowan Counties both Scotch Irish strongholds, "More hostile to England than any other in America." Two local leaders, Thomas Sumter, the "Carolina Gamecock" and Francis Marian of Huguenot stock, known as the "Swamp Fox" had nothing to learn from the English in matters of cruelty.

Andrew Pockets, the Presbyterian elder from Fort Ninety Six, turned to guerrilla warfare when his home was burnt. He was joined by William Davie and his "Bloody Corps", and William Lee Davidson from the Catawba bottom lands. Davie attacked but failed to dislodge a British post at Rocky Mount in July, but was successful at Hanging Rock with Thomas Sumter 12 miles east. Here the battle was bitter between Patriots and Loyalists; no British soldiers were engaged. The Patriots plundered the stores and got drunk, but that was what soldiers do. In August, still in the area, Tarleton struck back at Fishing Creek. Finding Sumter's force bathing, his cavalry killed 150 and captured 300. The whole country between the Rivers Peedee and Santee were in rebellion.

Horatio Gates, the British born general, who shared command

at Saratoga with Benedict Arnold, was put in command of the South by Congress, against Washington's advice, and he set out to retake Camden. His troops were short of food *and* rum. Gates assumed the town was for the taking, and the armies met at Rawdon by way of Gum Swamp. It was by accident, in the dark that they met, in fact, they all but collided, putting Gates in disarray and not knowing what to do. In the early morning, after some skirmishing, the British went in with the musket and the bayonet, which put the militia to flight, then followed on with the cavalry to finish off the regular troops. Cornwallis drove Gates to flight and disgrace, leaving hundreds of dead and wounded on the battlefield. Gates did not stop until he reached Hillsborough, 180 miles to the North East; reached in the respectable time of three days. He was replaced by Nathanael Greene, who had been Washington's choice in the first place.

As Cornwallis moved North his left flank was protected by Major Ferguson. Though badly wounded at Brandy Wine in front of Philadelphia, he played a big part in winning that battle with his rifle companies of Loyalist sharp-shooters. He had raised seven battalions of Loyalists and had been much angered by Colonel Tarleton's conduct of war. Hearing that an American force under Colonels John Sevier, William Campbell and Isaac Shelby, was moving towards him and greatly outnumbering his own Loyalists by at least two to one, he fell back towards Charlotte, taking up a position on King's Mountain. The Americans, mostly from Sullivan, Burke, Rutherford, Washington, Wilkes and Surrey Counties, all of North Carolina Scotch Irish territory, advanced through dripping woods, and caught Ferguson unprepared. Ferguson, with only one good arm, led from the front. On inspection later, his body was found to have received seven bullets and both his arms were broken. Loyalist casualties were 157 dead, 163 wounded and 698 prisoners and Ferguson was the only non-American in the battle. Hatreds were local and savage. Campbell tried to issue an order forbidding the killing of wounded and prisoners.

Except for local raids and forays, there was no major battle for the rest of the year; and Washington was in his winter quarters at New Windsor on the Hudson, which seemed to be a long way from the location of the next year's campaigning, in the South. Perhaps it

Andrew Jackson

Andrew Jackson was only fourteen when he witnessed the battles of Hanging Rock and Hobkirk's Hill, but he remembered enough to pass on his recollections to Francis Blair.

I was in one skirmish – that of Sands House – and there they caught me, along with my brother Robert and my cousin, Tom Crawford. A lieutenant of Tarleton's Light Dragoons tried to make me clean his boots and cut my arm with his sabre when I refused. After that they kept me in jail at Camden about two months, starved me nearly to death and gave me the smallpox. Finally my mother succeeded in persuading them to release Robert and me on account of our extreme youth and illness. Then Robert died of smallpox and I barely escaped death. When it left me I was a skeleton – not quite six feet long and a little over six inches thick! It took me all the rest of that year [1781] to recover my strength and get flesh enough to hide my bones. By that time Cornwallis had surrendered and the war was practically over in our part of the country.

I was never regularly enlisted, being only fourteen when the war practically ended. Whenever I took the field it was with Colonel Davie, who never put me in the ranks, but used me as a mounted orderly or messenger, for which I was well fitted, being a good rider and knowing all the roads in that region. The only weapons I had were a pistol that Colonel Davie gave me and a small fowling-piece that my Uncle Crawford lent to me. This was a light gun and would kick like sixty when loaded with a three-quarter-ounce ball or with nine buckshot. But it was a smart little gun and would carry the ball almost as true as a rifle fifteen or twenty rods, and threw the buckshot spitefully at close quarters – which was the way I used it in the defence of Captain Sands's house, where I was captured.

I was sorry about losing the gun there as about the loss of my own liberty, because Uncle Crawford set great store by the gun, which he had brought with him from the old country; and, besides, it was the finest in that whole region. Not long afterwards – while I was still in the Camden jail or stockade – some of Colonel Davie's men under Lieutenant Curriton captured a squad of Tories, one of whom had that gun in his possession, together with my pistol that Colonel Davie had given to me. This Tory's name was Mulford. The gun and pistol cost him his life. Davie's men regarded his possession of them as prima facie evidence that he had been a member of the party that captured Captain Sands's house, sacked and burned it and insulted the womenfolks of his family. He pleaded that he was not there; that he had bought the gun and pistol from another Tory. Davie's men told him it would do him no good to add lying to his other crimes, hanged him forthwith and afterward restored the gun and pistol to their proper owners.

was as well he had remained in the East as trouble was brewing. Six regiments of the Pennsylvanian Line, unpaid, ill-clothed and ill-fed, mutinied on New Year's Day, when they learned that money was being paid as a bounty to new recruits. Three were executed by firing squad. A revolt followed in the Jersey Line and the leaders were shot.

1781: In January General Greene sent Colonel David Morgan, another Saratogan hero, with his riflemen to the West of Catawba in South Carolina, along with a 1000 other troops, to cause mayhem, and give protection to local patriots. At Fort Ninety Six, 250 Loyalists were attacked and 150 killed or wounded. Cornwallis sent Tarleton with 1200 men in pursuit, but Morgan took a stand at Cowpens. He was a fine intelligent leader, always moving among his soldiers; telling them to pick out the British officers, and he designed a most unorthodox defensive layout of his men. Raw recruits of unknown quality at the front, seasoned campaigners behind them with instructions to shoot any man at the front who broke ranks. So when Tarleton drove head on with the bayonet, the line held. The Americans remained steady under fire and only Tarleton and his cavalry escaped. The British in one hour lost 1000 dead, wounded or captured and the Tarleton legend broken; the date was 17th January.

Morgan retreated to join Greene at the Dan River, just over the Virginian border. Cornwallis, with 2,500 men, chased after him; telling his officers to burn all unnecessary stores including the rum, transforming his force into a light corps and marched to Hillsborough, where the force rested. Cornwallis was now dangerously exposed; 250 miles from base with small chance of replacements of dead and wounded. The rains stopped, the dogwood was in blossom and Greene had received reinforcements. Battle was joined again in mid-March at Guilford Courthouse. It was Cowpens again, but the result was not the same. Both sides claimed victory but Cornwallis held the battlefield. He had 2,200 men and was heavily outnumbered by Greene, whose infantry did not break but were unable to counterattack. Cornwallis lost a quarter of his corps, saw no point in going on, and so returned South to the sea, harried all the way but with no losses in battle. It was another pyrrhic victory, at great cost. As Charles James Fox said in the

London Parliament, echoing Clinton after Bunker Hill "Another such victory would destroy the British Army." Nathaniel Green had proved to be a more than competent general; and as he said "We fight, get beat, rise and fight again." If there was a difference between the armies, it was that the British soldiers could not go home; some of them had fought in every battle from Bunker Hill in June 1775 to Guilford Courthouse in March 1781; and the final battle had yet to come.

Eutaw Springs in September was the last battle before Yorktown and could be termed as a tie. It was fought about 50 miles north west of Charleston, again between Greene and Cornwallis, and again there were similarities with Cowpens. Firstly, the American militia held bravely; then the second line of regular troops drove the British back. Unfortunately, the Virginian and Maryland regulars could not resist the liquor found in the enemy camp, and drank themselves stupid. Whereupon the British re-formed and their cavalry drove the Americans into the woods in disorder; but Cornwallis again had heavy losses.

On 1ˢᵗ August, Cornwallis went North to occupy Yorktown on the Yorktown Peninsula, on the West side of the entrance to the Chesapeake Bay, and began to fortify it. He had only 7,000 against a combined American and French force of 15,000. The French had a large flotilla of frigates blockading from the sea under Admiral de Grasse. Meanwhile, Admiral Graves was hunting a French Fleet off fog-bound New England, without being told he should have been at Yorktown to deal with de Grasse, who had come from the Caribbean. The siege began on 28ᵗʰ September and the British were under heavy bombardment from the sea, and from the huge siege artillery, Washington had brought to Yorktown. On 16ᵗʰ October, Cornwallis attempted to evacuate across the York River to Gloucester but was defeated by heavy weather. On 17ᵗʰ October, having been bombarded for 24 hours from the siege guns and the 24 French warships, Cornwallis, to prevent anymore unnecessary bloodshed, decided the game was up and surrendered. The following letters were then exchanged.

Sir,

I propose a cessation of hostilities for twenty four hours, and that two officers be appointed by each side, to meet at Mr Moore's house to settle terms for the surrender of the posts of York and Gloucester.

I have the honor to be, etc

Cornwallis.

My Lord,

I have had the honor of receiving your Lordship's letter of this date. An ardent desire to spare the further effusion of blood will readily incline me to listen to such terms for the surrender of your posts of York and Gloucester as are admissible. I wish, previously to the meeting of commissioners that your Lordship's proposals in writing may be sent to the American lines, for which purpose a suspension of hostilities, during two hours from the delivery of this letter, will be granted.

I have the honour to be, etc

George Washington

On 19th October 1781, the surrender took place; the same day as Sir Henry Clinton finally set sail with a rescue fleet. He reached the Chesapeake, five days too late; for the second time. He was also too late at Saratoga. An unfortunate habit in a general.

The prominence of Presbyterian soldiers in the Revolutionary Army is noted by the historian J R Sizoo, "When Cornwallis was driven back to ultimate defeat at Yorktown, all the colonels in the Colonial Army but one were Presbyterian Elders, and more than a half of all the officers and soldiers of the American Army during the Revolution were Presbyterians." Whether or not Mr Sizoo was referring to the regular army or the militia forces is not clear. But nobody doubts that the Scotch Irish Presbyterian involvement in the American War of Independence was out of all proportion to their numbers in the Thirteen Colonies. In the future wars in which the United States of America were participants, including their own Civil War of 1861, the fact that many of their soldiers, sailors and airmen originated from a tiny part of a tiny island off the West coast of Britain, itself a small island, was less important or noticeable. And that is how the Scotch Irish would have wanted it.

THE SCOTCH IRISH - BREWED IN SCOTLAND, BOTTLED IN ULSTER, UNCORKED IN AMERICA.

Postscript

Two of Scotland's gifts to the world are whisky and golf; such huge contributions to civilised living from such a small country could be thought to be more than enough. The Scotch Irish Ulstermen who gave 250,000 or so to the burgeoning race of Americans gave even more, and out of proportion to their numbers.

In the political field, at least fourteen Presidents from Andrew Jackson in 1818 through Woodrow Wilson to the Bushes, father and son, were descendents of Ulster immigrants. No single group of immigrants (for all non-Native Americans were immigrants) gave greater support, vocally and by force of arms to win American freedom from British Rule.

In religion their devout, belligerent Presbyterian Calvinism set the standard for democratic Christianity, and open the doors for those other major dissenting branches of the Church, Methodism and Baptists to create the greatest evangelical Christian Community in the world; and the blessings of a Church disestablished from the State.

In the field of arms, their courage and fortitude protected the frontier, as an example to those who came after them. Their way of doing things did not always please the politicians safe at home in their beds; but the job has to be done and they did it alone. In doing so, they opened the way to the West and the final drive to the Pacific Ocean, which frequently required force of arms. Remember the Alamo; the Scotch Irish were *also* there. They were the archetypal frontiersmen.

Theodore Roosevelt in his "The Winning of the West" considers the Scotch Irish as dominant in the push to the West, the vanguard; and he attributed their contribution as much to their race as to their experiences before the Revolutionary War.

He says:

"That these Irish Presbyterians were a bold and hardy race is proved by their at once pushing past the settled regions, and plunging into the wilderness as the leaders of the white advance. They were the first and last set of immigrants to do this; all others have merely followed in the wake of their predecessors. But, indeed they were fitted to be Americans from the very start; they were kinsfolk of the Covenanters; they deemed it a religious duty to interpret their own Bible, and held for a divine right the election of their own clergy. For generations their whole ecclesiastic and scholastic systems had been fundamentally democratic. In the hard

life of the frontier they had lost much of their religion, and they had but scant opportunity to give their children the schooling in which they believed; but what few meeting-houses and school-houses there were on the border were theirs."

Some say one third of Washington's army was composed of Scotch Irish. One-third, one quarter, nobody denies they made a huge numerical contribution, especially to the victories in the Carolinas and Virginia. Officers from the rank of general downwards were extraordinary large in numbers, and many were Elders of the Church. In the Civil War of 1861 they gave whole-hearted support to President Lincoln; and to Jefferson Davis, President of the Southern Confederacy also. For how could it have been otherwise – an accident of fate had made them inhabitants of much of the South, and Loyalty made them soldiers, and brave soldiers, of General Robert E Lee. By then they were Americans through and through.

The spirit lives on in the bone and the blood even today, and certainly in Ulster, the land they quit for America. On the eve of the Iraq War in March 2003, Lieutenant Colonel Tim Collins, commanding officer of the Royal Irish Regiment, addressed his battalion thus:

We go to liberate, not to conquer. We will not fly our flags in their country. We are entering Iraq to free a people and the only flag which will be flown in that land is their own. Show respect for them. There are some who are alive at this moment who will not be alive shortly. Those who do not wish to go on that journey, we will not send. As for the others, I expect you to rock their world. Wipe them out if that is what they choose. But if you are ferocious in battle remember to be magnanimous in victory.

Iraq is steeped in history. It is the site of the Garden of Eden, of the Great Flood and the birthplace of Abraham. Tread lightly there. You will see things that no man could pay to see – and you will have to go a long way to find a more decent, generous and upright people than the Iraqis. You will be embarrassed by their hospitality even though they have nothing. Don't treat them as refugees for they are in their own country. Their children will be poor, in years to come they will know that the light of liberation in their lives was brought by you.

If there are casualties of war then remember that when they woke up and got dressed in the morning they did not plan to die this day. Allow them dignity in death. Bury them properly and mark their graves. It is my foremost intention to bring every single one of you out alive. But there may be people among us who will not see the end of this campaign. We will put them in their sleeping bags and send them back. There will be no time for sorrow. The enemy should be in no doubt that we are his nemesis and that we are bringing about his rightful destruction. There are many regional commanders who have stains on their souls and they are stoking the fires of hell for Saddam. He and his forces will be destroyed by this coalition for what they have done. As they die they will know their deeds have brought them to this place. Show them no pity.

It is a big step to take another human life. It is not to be done lightly. I know of men who have taken life needlessly in other conflicts. I can assure you they live with the mark of Cain upon them. If someone surrenders to you then remember they have that right in international law and ensure that one day they go home to their family. The ones who wish to fight, well, we aim to please. If you harm the regiment or its history by over-enthusiasm in killing or in cowardice, know it is your family who will suffer. You will be shunned unless your conduct is of the highest – for your deeds will follow you down through history. We will bring shame on neither our uniform or our nation.

Selected Further Reading

ANTHONY James   The English in Ireland
in the 18th Century

ARDAGH John   Ireland and the Irish

BOSTON Brian   Ulster in World War II

BOLTON Charles   Scotch Irish Pioneers

CHEPESUIK Ronald   The Scotch Irish

DAVIES Norman   Europe

DUDLEY-EDWARDS Ruth   The Faithful Tribe

DUNAWAY Wayland   The Scotch Irish
of Colonial Pennsylvania

FALLS Cyril   Birth of Ulster

FROUDE James   The Irish Rebellion 1641

GRIFFIN Patrick   People with No Name

HAYWARD Richard   Ulster and the City of Belfast

KENNY Billy   The Making of America

LEYBURN James   The Scotch Irish:
a Social History

LECKY W.E.H.   History of Ireland
in the 18th Century

McCONVILLE Michael   Ascendancy to Oblivion

MULHOLLAND Marc   The Longest War

O'TOOLE Jimmy   The Carlow Gentry

TANNER Marcus   Last of the Celts

WRIGHT Esmond   The Fire of Liberty

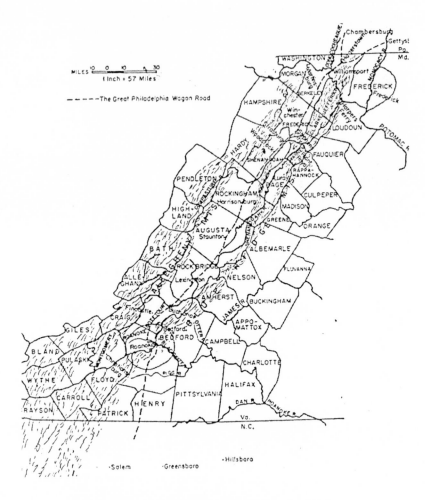

Valley of Virginia: Old and New Counties

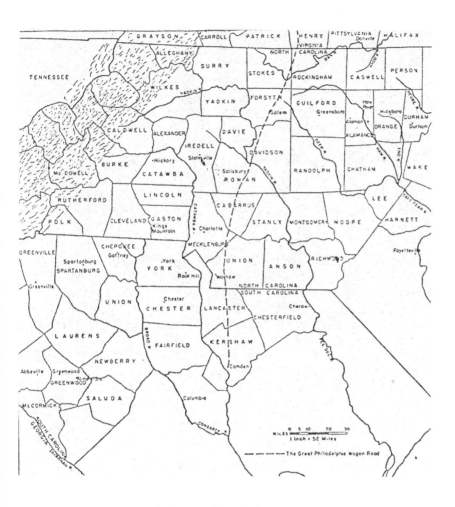

The Carolina Piedmont

The Battle of Brandywine

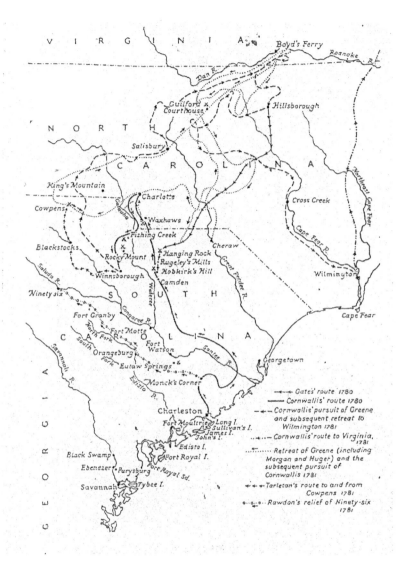

Legend (within map):

→→ Gates' route 1780
── Cornwallis' route 1780
─←─ Cornwallis' pursuit of Greene
    and subsequent retreat to
    Wilmington 1781
..←.. Cornwallis' route to Virginia,
    1781
...:...... Retreat of Greene (including
    Morgan and Huger) and the
    subsequent pursuit of
    Cornwallis 1781
←←← Tarleton's route to and from
    Cowpens 1781
o.o.o. Rawdon's relief of Ninety-six
    1781

Battles in the Carolinas

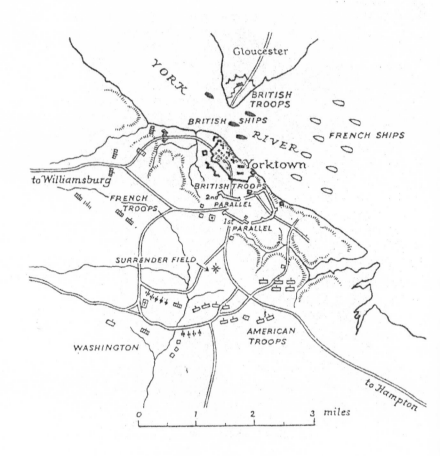

The siege of Yorktown

Index

Printed in the United Kingdom
by Lightning Source UK Ltd.
134462UK00002B/268-270/P